THE GOOD, THE BAD, AND THE UGLY
CLEVELAND INDIANS

THE GOOD, THE BAD, AND THE UGLY
CLEVELAND INDIANS

HEART-POUNDING, JAW-DROPPING, AND GUT-WRENCHING MOMENTS FROM CLEVELAND INDIANS HISTORY

Mary Schmitt Boyer

TRIUMPH
BOOKS

Triumph Books and colophon are registered trademarks of Random House, Inc.

Library of Congress Cataloging-in-Publication Data

Boyer, Mary Schmitt.
  The good, the bad, and the Ugly Cleveland Indians : heart-pounding, jaw-dropping, and gut-wrenching moments from Cleveland Indians history / Mary Schmitt Boyer.
    p. cm.
  Includes bibliographical references.
  ISBN-13: 978-1-60078-047-9
  ISBN-10: 1-60078-047-4
  1. Cleveland Indians (Baseball team)—History. I. Title.

GV875.C7B68 2008
796.357'640977132—dc22

2007051774

This book is available in quantity at special discounts for your group or organization. For further information, contact:

Triumph Books
542 South Dearborn Street
Suite 750
Chicago, Illinois 60605
(312) 939-3330
Fax (312) 663-3557

Printed in U.S.A.
ISBN: 978-1-60078-047-9
Design by Patricia Frey
Photos courtesy of AP/World Wide Photos unless otherwise indicated.

For Gene: It's all good.

CONTENTS

Foreword xi

Acknowledgments xiii

Introduction xv

The Good 1
    The Newest Star 1
    The Indians' First Championship 7
    Champions Again 11
    "A Beautiful Place to Play Ball" 14
    A Ray of Sunshine 17

The Bad 21
    Snow Days 21
    Two Outs Away 29
    Trader Lane 31

The Ugly 36
    A Black Eye for the Franchise 36
    An Angry Man 41
    Big Losers 47

In the Clutch   52

    Saving Grace   52

    Grace Under Pressure   57

    More Clutch Performers   61

Numbers Don't Lie (Or Do They?)   64

    Homers Are a Hit   64

    A Great Bargain   70

    Mass Appeal   77

It's Not Over 'Til It's Over   79

    The Indians' Greatest Comeback   79

    On the Other Hand   83

    Two More Games for the Ages   89

Race Relations   97

    A Shining Example   97

    A Monumental Move   105

    Another Historic Debut   110

Take This Job and Shove It   113

    A Man of Mystery   113

    Calling Dr. Hardy   121

    Working for a Living   125

Soldier Boys   129

    Doing His Duty   129

    He Lived to Tell about It   132

    Patriotic Acts   138

Pain and Suffering 143

   Unspeakable Tragedy 143

   A Deadly Pitch 149

   A Career Cut Short 153

Answers 159

Notes 161

FOREWORD

Some books are like popcorn.

You read a few sentences. Then a page. Then a chapter.

It goes down easy, real easy. Almost too easy.

Before you know it, you've spent an hour with your head in a book reading about your favorite baseball team. And every few minutes, you say, "I remember that." Even better, you say, "I didn't know that."

Better yet, "So that was the real story."

That's what Mary Schmitt Boyer has done in her new book on the Cleveland Indians. This is not heavy duty history. It's not a book aimed at the numbers freaks who live to make up new statistics because the 10,000 we already have to measure players aren't enough.

This is a book for a fan who likes a big box of popcorn while at a game. It's for the fan who talks to a relative or a friend between pitches and innings—telling stories of Tribe games and teams from long ago—or maybe still second-guessing the manager for a move he made last week. It's for the fan who discovered baseball before the Jacobs Field Era, or the young fan who just came to the game with C.C. Sabathia and wants to know more about the team that he has suddenly come to love.

The Good.

The Bad.

The Ugly.

The Cleveland Indians.

Somehow, that title does fit our Tribe.

It's so nice when the good arrives. For all the agony of that last, lost weekend at Fenway Park in Boston in the American League Championship Series, the 2007 Indians did win 96 games. They did knock off New York in the first round. They were the only team to beat Boston in any games in the postseason. More important, they were entertaining—and showed that the Indians had come out of the coma that had stifled the franchise for several years after fun run of the new stadium and the Tribe of the 1990s.

But this book also takes us back to 1920 and 1948, when the Indians actually made the World Series and won! Those are two teams worth getting to know. There are some of usual suspects for the ugly—beer night, Albert Belle, and the author throws in a few more.

Take this book on a plane, to beach, or to your favorite chair. Maybe fire up some popcorn. Just relax, and page through it. This is the kind of book with chapters that don't have to be read in order, but soon, you'll be nibbling away at most pages—and be hungry for more.

—Terry Pluto

ACKNOWLEDGMENTS

B ooks like this can only be completed with the help of many, including all those in the Indians organization, especially Mark Shapiro, Bart Swain, and Curtis Danberg.

Thanks to my colleagues at *The Plain Dealer*, especially my bosses, Roy Hewitt, Mike Starkey, and Dave Campbell, columnists Bill Livingston, Terry Pluto, and Bud Shaw, and the fabulous Paul Hoynes. Burt Graeff, Dennis Manoloff, Bob Dolgan, and Russ Schneider always have time to help, as did Mary Ellen Kollar and David Furyes at the main branch of the Cleveland Public Library.

In researching this book, I read all or parts of the following works: *The Cleveland Indians Encyclopedia*, Third Edition, *Tribe Memories: The First Century*, and *The Boys of the Summer of '48*, all by Russell Schneider; *Veeck—As In Wreck: The Autobiography of Bill Veeck* by Bill Veeck with Ed Linn; *Indian Summer: The Forgotten Story of Louis Sockalexis, the First Native American in Major League Baseball* by Brian McDonald; *Now Pitching, Bob Feller: A Baseball Memoir* by Bob Feller with Bill Gilbert; *Bob Feller's Little Black Book of Baseball Wisdom* by Bob Feller with Burton Rocks; *Moe Berg: Athlete, Scholar, Spy* by Louis Kaufman, Barbara Fitzgerald, and Tom Sewell; *The Curse of Rocky Colavito: A Loving Look at a Thirty-Year Slump* by Terry Pluto, and *Heroes, Scamps, and Good Guys: 101 Colorful Characters from Cleveland Sports History* by Bob Dolgan. Many thanks to all the authors for their insights.

INTRODUCTION

The good. The bad. The ugly. That just about covers the 2007 Cleveland Indians' season. So much good was overshadowed by the ugly ending, when the Indians built a 3–1 lead in games against the Boston Red Sox in the American League Championship Series only to lose three straight games and their chance to advance to the World Series for the first time since 1997.

They were outscored in those three games, 30–5. If that wasn't bad enough, they awoke on the morning of Game 7 to reports that pitcher Paul Byrd had spent $25,000 on human growth hormone. Byrd told reporters he had a doctor's prescription for the drug to treat an adult growth hormone deficiency.

It was a disheartening end to what had been a terrific season. After all, the Indians did finish the regular season with a 96–66 record, tying those Red Sox for the best record in baseball. They won their first AL Central Division crown since 2001 and beat the archrival New York Yankees in the AL Division Series to advance to the ALCS for the first time since 1998.

C.C. Sabathia won the AL Cy Young Award, while Fausto Carmona finished fourth in the Cy Young voting after exploding onto the scene and finished with a 19–8 record and a 3.06 ERA. Rafael Bentancourt and Rafael Perez became two of the best set-up men in baseball, and closer Joe Borowski led the AL with 45 saves, even if he did always seem to do it the hard way.

Sabathia, center fielder Grady Sizemore, and catcher Victor Martinez were all named to the All-Star team. Sizemore won a Gold Glove and finished fourth in the league in runs scored with 118, fifth in walks with 101, and sixth in stolen bases with 33. Martinez had a career year with a .301 batting average, 114 RBIs, 25 home runs, and 40 doubles.

Eric Wedge was named AL Manager of the Year, and Mark Shapiro was named Executive of the Year.

Every move the team made seemed to work, whether it was bringing back 40-year-old Kenny Lofton or inserting rookie Asdrubal Cabrera at second base. With things going so well during the season, Wedge and designated hitter Travis Hafner each signed contract extensions.

Somehow the team whose first home series was snowed out and whose second home series was moved to the covered stadium in Milwaukee finished the season red hot.

Then came the collapse in Boston, where Sabathia, Carmona, and Hafner failed to come through and the Tribe's best chance to tie the score at 3–3 in Game 7 was lost when third base coach Joel Skinner held up a streaking Lofton at third after a ball off the bat of Franklin Gutierrez caromed off the stands behind third base and wound up in left field. The Indians ended up losing the game, 11–2, but at the time the shift in momentum was palpable.

Indians fans who had gathered in Jacobs Field to watch the game in Fenway Park groaned. Their hopes had been dashed again. But they are a sturdy bunch. The pain from the loss will lessen as time goes on, and their hearts will heal. They will regain faith in their team just about the time spring training rolls around. Then it will be Tribe Time again.

THE GOOD

THE NEWEST STAR

Cleveland fans were on to Grady Sizemore long before the national media caught up.

Well, female Cleveland fans, at least.

Before Sizemore made the All-Star team and the cover of *Sports Illustrated,* his fan club, Grady's Ladies, showed their devotion by wearing pink T-shirts, and "Mrs. Sizemore" T-shirts were one of the most popular items in the team's gift shops.

Shortly after the Cleveland Browns drafted former Notre Dame quarterback Brady Quinn in the spring of 2007, Cleveland's *Plain Dealer* ran a funny story in its irreverent pdQ section about which of the two "hunkiest dreamboats" was a better catch. Sizemore won, partly because he is already an established star and partly because he's a tad older and, theoretically, closer to wanting to settle down.

The article referred to Sizemore as a "stud muffin" and Quinn as "beefcake." And just in case you're wondering, the story was written by a man. A man who is a huge sports fan, but still...

Like many sports stars, Sizemore took full advantage when opportunity knocked at his door. He was slated for Triple A Buffalo in the 2005 season, but when Juan Gonzalez got hurt during spring training, Sizemore was called up. He had a breakout season with a .289 average in 158 games, 37 doubles, 11 triples, 22 home runs, and 22 stolen bases.

Then in the disappointing season of 2006, which started with so much promise and ended with a 78–84 record, Sizemore's selection to the All-Star team was one of the first-half highlights, and he put together one of the best seasons in the club's history. He led the Major League in runs scored with 134, and extra-base hits with 92 (the third highest total in team history and the highest total for the team's leadoff hitter), and led the AL in doubles with 53. He was second in the league with 349 total bases. He became the first Indian to hit double figures in doubles, triples, home runs, and stolen bases in two seasons, and he was only the second major leaguer to post more than 50 doubles, 10 triples, 20 homers, and 20 steals in the same season.

He was a model of consistency, playing in every game and setting a team record for fewest double plays grounded into—two.

Indians fans knew Grady Sizemore was a future star long before the national media caught on.

GRADY SIZEMORE'S ALL-STAR STATISTICS

Year	AB	R	H	E	RBI	Avg
2006	2	0	0	0	0	.000
2007	1	0	0	0	0	.000
Totals	3	0	0	0	0	.000

His 419 total chances were the most in the majors and his 655 at-bats were the fifth highest in team history. He also was named the Indians' Man of the Year by the Cleveland baseball writers.

While pointing out all that in the team's press guide, even the Indians admitted, "Okay, we're gushing now."

The funny thing was, when Sizemore came to the Indians on June 27, 2002, as part of the trade that sent pitchers Bartolo Colon and Tim Drew—along with cash to Montreal—he wasn't the focal point. Instead, the media made more of promising minor league infielder Brandon Phillips or left-hander Cliff Lee.

General manager Mark Shapiro certainly knew what he was getting, though.

"Each guy in the trade was an important piece, and the trade would not have been completed by us without all three included," said Shapiro, who also got veteran first baseman Lee Stevens in the deal. "In fact, we were trying to get a fourth player added until Colon strained a muscle just before we completed the trade. More was made of Phillips and Lee because they were performing better and at higher levels (AAA and AA, respectively). Grady was having a mediocre season in A ball, but we loved his upside. He was the lone projection guy in the deal, but we felt he had a high upside. In all honesty, we felt Phillips was the surest thing in the deal. Looks like we were right on him but not on our time frame, unfortunately. He was the highest regarded prospect in the industry at the time of the trade, but Grady was no secret and was an important part of the deal."

After several seasons shuttling between Cleveland and its Triple A affiliate in Buffalo, in 2006 Phillips was traded to

Cincinnati, where he became the Reds' starting second baseman. Five days earlier, the Indians signed Sizemore to a $31.45 million, seven-year contract extension, including a club option that could keep him with the team through 2012. If he continues to play as he has been, he'll be a steal at that price. He was selected to his second All-Star Game in 2007, about six weeks after appearing on the cover of *Sports Illustrated* with the headline, "Why Sizemore Matters."

In the article, writer Tom Verducci quotes assorted baseball executives raving about Sizemore, including Shapiro.

INDIANS EXTRA-BASE HITS LEADERS

1. Albert Belle, 103, 1995
2. Hal Trosky, 96, 1936
3. Grady Sizemore, 92, 2006

"To watch him play day in and day out is a rare treat," Shapiro told the magazine. "All of us, from the front office to the players to the bat boys, are fortunate to see him every day. He is without a doubt one of the greatest players of our generation."

Shapiro likened Sizemore to New York Yankees star Derek Jeter because of his popularity, his approach, and his athleticism. (And like Jeter, Sizemore is biracial. His father is African American; his mother is white.)

White Sox manager Ozzie Guillen, who picked Sizemore as a 2006 All-Star reserve, called the Indians center fielder "the best player in our league" and "Superman." Toronto manager John Gibbons said, "He's the kind of player every manager wants. He can do it all, but what's so great is he plays the game the right way and he gives your team energy every day. He's a dirtbag. He'll do whatever he can to beat you."

Like stealing home in a 9–3 victory at Toronto on August 26, 2005, with two strikes on Travis Hafner.

"I didn't know what he was doing," Hafner told reporters after the game. "I thought maybe he had to run to the bathroom or something. If I had swung and hit Grady in the face, I would have had every woman in America mad at me."

Sizemore doesn't seem overly impressed with the effect he seems to have on members of the female persuasion.

"You can never complain about being liked by the fans," Sizemore told the *Akron Beacon Journal*. "It's kind of funny to see little girls with the [pink Mrs. Sizemore] T-shirts, but it's more for the fans."

Then again, he doesn't seem overly impressed with himself in general. If there is such a thing as a reluctant superstar, Sizemore is it.

"I was at the All-Star Game with him last year [2006]," Toronto third baseman Troy Glaus told *Sports Illustrated*, "and I'm telling you, he did not say one word the entire time. Not one word. And it's not because he's a bad guy. He's just that quiet."

Sizemore really was thrilled to make his first All-Star team.

HOT STREAK

One of the highlights of the Indians' 2007 season was the 26-game hitting streak by Casey Blake, tied for the sixth longest streak in team history. It lasted from May 20 to June 18. Ironically, Blake went hitless as the Indians pounded the Philadelphia Phillies for 11 hits in a 10–1 victory. He was in the on-deck circle when Josh Barfield flied out to center for the third out in the eighth inning.

"It was interesting," Blake told reporters after the game. "When you don't have a hit in a streak like this, the anxiety builds the whole game, especially when the game's out of hand. You're like, 'Whatever I do isn't going to matter, but I'd like to get a hit.'"

Blake went 33 for 104 during the streak (.317), with seven home runs and 18 RBIs. Twelve times his hit came in the sixth inning or later.

Although it was fun while it lasted, Blake admitted he was no threat to Joe DiMaggio's record 56-game hitting streak.

"You want it to last as long as you can, but 56 games? Are you kidding me?" Blake told reporters. "I told myself, 'What are you fretting about?'"

"It's exciting," he told reporters. "I never really thought about it. I've just been focusing on the season. Everyone should want to play well enough to make the All-Star team, but I didn't expect this. It wasn't one of my goals, something I wrote down in a book."

But a few days before he was named to the 2007 squad as a reserve, Sizemore said he wouldn't be disappointed if he didn't make it again.

"I think it's great if you make it," he said. "If you don't, it's no big deal either. I haven't even thought about it, to be honest with you. I don't focus on that. There's so much going on day to day in the baseball season, it's the last thing on my mind. That's all great. That's all fun. But that's not what I think about. That's not what I enjoyed the most about being an All-Star. Being part of the game and playing with those guys. All that other stuff is stuff I'm not really accustomed to."

He's referring to all the hype and hoopla that surround the game, including mass media sessions, parades over red carpets, and exaggerated introductions. The things he seemed happiest about were that he was voted onto the team by his peers—and that he would be joined by teammates Victor Martinez and C.C. Sabathia.

TRIVIA

Who is the only other major league player besides Grady Sizemore to hit at least 50 doubles, 10 triples, 20 homers, and 20 steals in the same season?

Find the answers on pages 159–160.

"It will be nice to have somebody to talk to and share the experience with," said Sizemore, who turned down a chance to compete in the home-run derby the day before the All-Star Game. "I didn't know too many of those guys last year."

Sizemore grew up in a close family outside Seattle, in the northern suburb of Mill Creek in Snohomish County. Snohomish County also happened to be the home of Indians Hall of Fame center fielder Earl Averill, a native of Everett. In fact, according to *Sports Illustrated*, when *The Herald* recently compiled a list of the county's top 50 athletes, Averill was number one and Sizemore was number 16.

Sizemore's father, Grady Sizemore II, was an insurance adjuster who played baseball at Mars Hill College in North Carolina. His mother, Donna, was a bookkeeper. They have another son, Corey, two years younger than Grady. The boys were always playing one sport or another, and Grady usually won. He was a three-sport star at Cascade High School, but he worked on his studies, too, and never got the sort of big head so many prep stars do.

"I don't ever recall seeing Grady walk down the middle of the hallway and expecting the seas to part," former Cascade baseball coach Bob Smithson told the *Akron Beacon Journal.*

INDIANS TOP HITTING STREAKS

31 games:	Nap Lajoie, 1906
30 games:	Sandy Alomar, 1997
29 games:	Bill Bradley, 1902
28 games:	Joe Jackson, 1911
	Hal Trosky, 1936
27 games:	Dale Mitchell, 1953
26 games:	Harry Bay, 1902
	Casey Blake, 2007
24 games:	Matt Williams, 1997

He was good enough in football that former University of Washington coach Rick Neuheisel offered him a scholarship to play quarterback for the Huskies. But when the Montreal Expos gave him a $2 million signing bonus, college—and football—took a back seat.

"I'm sure he'd be in the NFL right now if he weren't playing baseball," Shapiro told *Sports Illustrated.* "He's that kind of elite athlete. The game needs more like him."

THE INDIANS' FIRST CHAMPIONSHIP

It never looked as if 1920 was going to be the Indians' year.

Instead, it appeared it would be best remembered for the tragic death of shortstop Ray Chapman, who was hit in the head by a pitch from Carl Mays of the Yankees on August 16 in New York and died the next day—the only major league player ever fatally wounded during a game.

But the Indians regrouped, first using reserve infielder Harry Lunte and then calling up Joe Sewell from the minor leagues when Lunte hurt his leg, and continued to push toward the post-season. They had finished second to Boston and Chicago, respectively, in 1918 and 1919, and player-manager Tris Speaker had them one game ahead of Chicago in the last week of the 1920 regular season when seven players on the defending champion White Sox were suspended for conspiring to fix the 1919 World Series. Cleveland won three of its last five games and finished two games ahead of Chicago, setting up a best-of-nine World Series against the Brooklyn Dodgers. Sewell, who was not on the roster September 1, won an appeal to be able to play.

Game 1, Tuesday, October 5. Cleveland 3, at Brooklyn 1—Catcher Steve O'Neill had two doubles and two runs batted in to back the five-hit pitching of Stan Coveleski on a cold and windy day before a chilled crowd of 23,573 in Ebbets Field. Coveleski walked just one and held the Dodgers scoreless through six innings.

"Coveleski pitched excellent ball today," Speaker told reporters after the game. "With the wind blowing as hard as it was, he worked under a handicap but he delivered in the pinches, and that is what counts. He was never nervous. It was just a ballgame with him. He pitched a typical Coveleski game.

"The result of the game goes to show that I was not boasting when I contended that Cleveland would display just as good pitching as Brooklyn. They would have us believe that Brooklyn has the real pitching market cornered. It is my belief that the pitching in the American League is every bit as good as that in the National, and our batting average of .302 [for the regular season] was deservedly earned."

Game 2, Wednesday, October 6. At Brooklyn 3, Cleveland 0—Burleigh Grimes held the Indians scoreless and didn't allow a runner past second base until the eighth inning as the Dodgers evened up the series before a crowd of 22,559.

"I give Grimes the credit," Speaker told reporters after the game. "He is a good pitcher. He has a great spitball."

Game 3, Thursday, October 7. At Brooklyn 2, Cleveland 1—The Dodgers jumped on Ray Caldwell for two runs in the first inning, and left-hander Sherry Smith limited Cleveland to three hits. The Indians scored their only run when Speaker raced home from second after his double rolled through the legs of left fielder Zach Wheat in the fourth inning.

"The clubs are very evenly matched, but I think we have the edge on Cleveland in respect to pitchers," Brooklyn manager Wilbert "Uncle Robbie" Robinson told reporters after the game. "The thing needed in a World Series is nerve, and our boys certainly have plenty of it."

Game 4, Saturday, October 9. At Cleveland 5, Brooklyn 1—This time it was the Indians' turn to jump out to a quick lead. Brooklyn right-hander Leon Cadore found himself trailing, 2–0, in the first inning, and another five-hitter by Coveleski helped the Indians knot the series and provided a successful outcome in the first World Series game to be played in Cleveland.

TRIVIA

Why didn't the 1920 World Series start in Cleveland?

Find the answers on pages 159–160.

Game 5, Sunday, October 10. At Cleveland 8, Brooklyn 1—It was quite a day for the Indians and their fans. Bill Wambsganss made the only unassisted triple play in World Series history, pitcher Jim Bagby became the first pitcher to hit a home run in the World Series, and Elmer Smith became the first player to hit a grand slam in the World Series as the Indians, behind Smith's first-inning blast off Grimes, routed the Dodgers.

The Dodgers had runners on first and second in the fifth inning when pitcher Clarence Mitchell, who relieved Grimes, lined a shot toward center field. Wambsganss caught it, stepped on second to double up Pete Kilduff, and then tagged out Otto Miller as he approached second base.

"It was one of the most remarkable games I ever took part in," Speaker told reporters after the game. "I am especially proud of Bill Wambsganss. I am happy for his sake. I trust what he did yesterday will silence the criticism of him forever. Bill is a great player. Any team in the country would be glad to have him."

Game 6, Monday, October 11. At Cleveland 1, Brooklyn 0—Walter "Duster" Mails pitched his way out of a bases-loaded jam

DID YOU KNOW...

That as a reward for winning the 1920 World Series, the players each got a new contract and a bonus worth 10 days' pay, and manager Tris Speaker got an engraved gold watch? The players gave owner Jim Dunn diamond-studded cuff links.

in the second inning and threw a three-hitter as the Indians moved within a game of their first World Series championship. Cleveland scored its only run on a two-out single by Speaker in the sixth inning and a double by George Burns.

Game 7, Tuesday, October 12. At Cleveland 3, Brooklyn 0—Coveleski tied a major league record by recording his third victory in one World Series, and the Indians shut out the Dodgers for the second straight game to win their first baseball championship before a deliriously happy crowd of 27,525 at League Park. The Indians got the only run they needed in the fourth inning, on a throwing error by Grimes, who was working on only two days' rest. They tacked on single runs in the fifth and seventh. At the end of the game, fans swarmed onto the field to celebrate.

"From the start, I never had any doubt of our being able to win the championship of the world," Speaker told reporters after the game. "The American League campaign was what gave us the trouble, but the fact that we had to fight it right out to the finish helped us against Brooklyn. We were playing at top speed when the regular season ended and kept going the same gait until we had won the world's title.

"All the boys have felt the same way. They know they are a good ball club and have known it right along. When we lost two in a row in Brooklyn, none of us was discouraged for we knew we had a better ballclub than Brooklyn and would win if all the breaks were not against us."

Robinson told reporters after the game, "Cleveland has a wonderful ballclub, and Tris Speaker and his men certainly deserve the splendid support they have received from the city. It was a well-fought and honestly played Series. We did our best, but we couldn't hit Cleveland pitching."

CHAMPIONS AGAIN

It was all about Boston for the Indians in 1948.

When Cleveland lost to Detroit, 7–1, and Boston beat New York, 10–5, on the last day of the season, the Indians and the Red Sox finished atop the American League with identical 96–58 records, forcing the first AL championship playoff game.

The next day, October 4, Ken Keltner hit a three-run home run in the fourth inning and rookie left-hander Gene Bearden pitched a five-hitter on one day's rest to lift the Indians to an 8–3 victory that clinched the AL pennant. Lou Boudreau went 4-for-4 with two home runs to help the Indians advance to the World Series for the first time since 1920. Their opponent? The Boston Braves.

Game 1, Wednesday, October 6. At Boston 1, Cleveland 0—Bob Feller actually outpitched Johnny Sain, allowing just two hits to Sain's four, but a controversial umpire's call in the eighth inning allowed pinch runner Phil Masi to score the game's only run.

"It was a tough one for Feller to lose and a great game for Sain to win, but that's always the way," Boston manager Billy Southworth told reporters after the game.

Feller walked catcher Bill Salkeld to lead off the inning. Masi ran for him and went to second on a sacrifice. Eddie Stanky was

ATTENDANCE FIGURES DURING 1948 WORLD SERIES

Game 1 at Boston—40,135
Game 2 at Boston—39,633
Game 3 at Cleveland—70,306
Game 4 at Cleveland—81,897
Game 5 at Cleveland—86,288
Game 6 at Boston—40,103

intentionally walked to set up the double play. Feller threw to Boudreau to try and pick off Masi, but umpire Bill Stewart called Masi safe, although photos seemed to indicate Masi was out. Feller got Sain to fly out, but Tommy Holmes singled to drive in Masi.

"I'm sure that Masi was out," Boudreau told reporters after the game. "Stewart is a National League umpire, and he is not acquainted with our pickoff play. I don't think he was in a good position to see the tag. I know I got him."

According to author Russell Schneider in the third edition of *The Cleveland Indians Encyclopedia,* years later Masi told Feller that Boudreau had, in fact, tagged him out. Masi also told Feller that Stewart had admitted to him in private that he'd made a mistake.

Game 2, Thursday, October 7. Cleveland 4, at Boston 1— Player-manager Lou Boudreau and center fielder Larry Doby each had a double and an RBI, and Bob Lemon sprinkled eight hits over nine innings as the Indians rebounded with a 4–1 victory to tie the Series. Ironically, Lemon's throw to Boudreau picked off Earl Torgeson on the same pickoff play in the first inning.

"Still no prediction on how long it's going to last," Boudreau told reporters after the game. "Just going along as we have all season—out to win the game coming up."

Lemon said to reporters after the game, "The toughest thing for me the last few days has been sitting on the bench with the pennant at stake. That would give a guy ulcers a lot faster than pitching. Sure, there were a few butterflies in my stomach when I walked out there for the first inning, but they disappeared with the first pitch."

DID YOU KNOW...

That Hall of Famer Lou Boudreau had his best season during the Indians' 1948 championship season? Boudreau, the team's manager and shortstop, hit .355 with 18 home runs and 106 RBIs. He walked 98 times and struck out just nine times in 560 at-bats.

Game 3, Friday, October 8. At Cleveland 2, Boston 0—Left-handed knuckleballer Gene Bearden almost beat the Braves by himself. The former first baseman allowed just five hits and had two of the Indians' five hits, including a double, as Cleveland took a 2–1 lead in the Series.

"Always wanted Gene to be a pitcher, but it took a lot of persuading," Bearden's father, Henry, told reporters after the game. "Finally got him off first base and on to the mound, but he still likes hitting just about as well as pitching. Didn't look bad with the stick today, either."

Said Southworth to reporters, "We'll be back with Johnny Sain to even it up. This won't get the boys down. They don't lose that easily."

Game 4, Saturday, October 9. At Cleveland 2, Boston 1—The Indians jumped on Sain for a run in the first inning, and Doby hit a 410-foot home run in the third. Steve Gromek's seven-hitter allowed the lead to stand and the Indians moved a game from their second World Series title. Marv Rickert's seventh-inning home run was all the Braves could muster.

"I didn't sleep much last night," Gromek told reporters after the game. "I still was nervous taking my warmup pitches. But when the first batter flied out, it was just another game until the ninth.... When I was out there for the ninth, I was thinking about this being the Series and my biggest chance as a pitcher and I believe I threw the ball faster than ever before."

Stewart, the umpire who made the controversial safe call on Masi in the first game, was escorted off the field by several policemen after Game 4. He had called Boudreau out at third after Boudreau tried to stretch a double into a triple. Stewart also called Boston's Alvin Dark safe at a close play at first base in Game 2.

Game 5, Sunday, October 10. Boston 11, at Cleveland 5—Boston third baseman Bob Elliott hit two home runs as the Braves pummeled the Indians for 12 hits before a disappointed World Series–record crowd of 86,288. Every player in the Braves lineup had at least one hit, including starting pitcher Nels Potter. Boston took a 3–0 lead in the first, but the Indians actually held a 5–4 lead after the fourth. The Braves settled things once and for all with six runs in the top of the seventh, making a winner out of Warren Spahn.

"What a relief to get some runs—and pitching, too," Southworth told reporters after the game. "Gosh, we really exploded. Yep, we're right back in this Series."

Game 6, Monday, October 11. Cleveland 4, at Boston 3—The Indians built a 4–1 lead in the eighth inning, but Boston kept things close with two runs in their half of the eighth. Lemon won his second game of the Series, with relief help by Bearden, who pitched his way out of a one-out, bases-loaded jam in the eighth inning.

"Oh, I was tired," Lemon told reporters after the game. "Lou did right in taking me out. We won, though. That's all I care about."

First baseman Eddie Robinson paced the Indians' offense with two hits and an RBI. Joe Gordon hit a solo home run in the sixth. It was quite a week for Bearden, who won the game that clinched a tie for the pennant, won the game that clinched the pennant, won one World Series game and saved another as the Indians won the World Series for the first time in 28 years.

"It was Bearden's Series all the way, all his," Boudreau told reporters after the game. "Gene was the key to our success."

"A BEAUTIFUL PLACE TO PLAY BALL"

It's hard to believe that Jacobs Field is approaching its 15th birthday.

The cozy little ballpark tucked into downtown Cleveland is every bit as charming as it was when it opened to much fanfare in 1994.

The public got its first look at the $169 million ballpark on April 2, 1994, when the Indians played host to the Pittsburgh Pirates in an exhibition game. The official grand opening came on April 4 in the season opener against the Seattle Mariners. President Bill Clinton threw out the first pitch, and although Randy Johnson threw a no-hitter for seven innings, the Indians eventually thrilled the 41,459 fans in attendance with a 4–3 victory on a single by Wayne Kirby in the eleventh inning.

Jacobs Field was an instant hit with fans when it opened in 1994 and hasn't lost a bit of its appeal 15 years later.

The park probably would have been a draw in and of itself, especially since it replaced the dank, drafty, cavernous Cleveland Municipal Stadium. But the new ballpark also ushered in a great new era of Indians baseball, one long-suffering Indians fans had been hoping for since the 1954 team was swept out of the World Series by the New York Giants.

Shortstop Omar Vizquel, obtained in a trade from Seattle in the off season, made his Cleveland debut the day Jacobs Field opened. Both became equally popular.

"When I first saw Jacobs Field a few days before the 1994 season opener, it knocked my socks off," Vizquel said in his 2002 autobiography, *Omar!: My Life On and Off the Field*. "Everything was first class. There wasn't one single feature that stood out; rather, it was the overall feel. It didn't remind me of any other ballpark; it was unique. It was just a beautiful place to play ball."

The park changed the landscape of downtown Cleveland, literally and figuratively. The Indians had been unhappy in the stadium for years, feuding constantly with either the city or Cleveland Browns owner Art Modell, whose Stadium Corporation

ALL-STAR GAMES IN CLEVELAND

- July 8, 1935, American League 4, National League 1 at Cleveland Municipal Stadium
- July 13, 1954, American League 11, National League 9 at Cleveland Municipal Stadium
- July 9, 1963, National League 5, American League 3 at Cleveland Municipal Stadium
- August 9, 1981, National League 5, American League 4 at Cleveland Municipal Stadium
- July 8, 1997, American League 3, National League 1 at Jacobs Field

took over operation of the stadium. In 1984, Cuyahoga County voters rejected a property tax increase to fund a new domed stadium. But the Indians' new owners, brothers Dick and David Jacobs, worked with civic leaders to come up with a plan for a public/private partnership that would result in a new baseball-only stadium, as well as a new basketball arena for the Cleveland Cavaliers. The Gateway Sports and Entertainment Complex, funded in part by a sin tax on cigarettes and alcohol, helped revitalize downtown Cleveland, although the Indians' departure from the stadium hastened the departure of the Browns for Baltimore after the 1995 season.

The Indians tried their best to fill the void left by the Browns with year after year of thrilling baseball. Fans swarmed to see them, and the team set a major league record with 455 sellouts from June 7, 1995, to April 2, 2001. Cleveland advanced to the World Series in 1995 and 1997 and played host to the All-Star Game on July 8, 1997, when Sandy Alomar Jr. of the Indians stole the show. With the score tied at 1–1 and two outs in the seventh inning, the Indians catcher hit a two-run home run to snap a three-game losing streak by the American League and send most of the stadium-record crowd of 44,916 home happy after the 3–1 victory. Alomar was named the game's Most Valuable Player in a vote of the media. He was the first Indian to win the award, and the only player to do so in his home park. He was the first Indian to hit a homer in the All-Star Game since Rocky Colavito did it in 1959.

Indians manager Mike Hargrove, Alomar, Jim Thome, and David Justice represented Cleveland. Kenny Lofton, then with the Atlanta Braves, played for the National League. Former Indian Albert Belle of the Chicago White Sox, booed mercilessly by the fans during his introduction, was named to the AL team but chose not to play.

Alomar, who was leading the American League with a .375 average and a 30-game hitting streak, was a reserve on the team, so he had only one at-bat. He made the most of it, lining a 2–2 pitch off loser Shawn Estes into the left-field bleachers. Bernie Williams, who walked and took second on a wild pitch, scored ahead of Alomar. Alomar's homer made a winner of Jose Rosado.

"I felt like I was flying," Alomar told reporters after the game. "I've never run the bases so fast on a home run. This is a dream I don't want to wake up from. You probably only get one chance to play an All-Star Game in your home stadium."

Said Estes to reporters after the game, "I kept his hitting streak alive. I wouldn't have picked anybody to hit a homer off me, but I'm happy for him that he did. It's a great time for him. Playing at home, the hitting streak, the fans obviously love him."

A RAY OF SUNSHINE

It was a cold and rainy Monday in Cleveland. The Indians were struggling on the road, and the fans were getting restless even though it was only a few weeks into the 2007 season.

Bill Livingston, the erudite sports columnist for *The Plain Dealer*, was a guest on the local cable television show *More Sports and Les Levine*. Midway through the hour-long show, Livingston informed host Levine that he thought it was possible popular shortstop Omar Vizquel could be back.

The switchboard lit up.

Livingston admitted it was more of a gut feeling, or maybe wishful thinking. He had no inside information, he said, only a dissatisfaction with the current state of the Indians infield—a portal to the outfield, he had called it in a recent column, borrowing the phrase from an equally dissatisfied fan.

While several callers voiced their enthusiasm for the notion, one realist asked why the Indians would be willing to pay Vizquel now that he was 40 years old when they weren't willing to pay to keep him when he was 37.

The killjoy.

The fact of the matter remains that the Gold Glove shortstop is as beloved as ever. The day before Livingston's appearance with Levine, longtime *Plain Dealer* sportswriter Paul Hoynes had selected Vizquel as the best shortstop he'd ever seen. To celebrate Hoynes's 25th season of covering the team, *The Plain Dealer* was running a series entitled "The Best I've Ever Seen." Hoynes named the best player he'd seen at each position in those 25 years.

"I've tried not to be a homer in picking the best players I've seen while writing about the Indians and Major League Baseball since 1983," Hoynes wrote. "Two of my first three choices, Eddie Murray and Roberto Alomar, made stops in Cleveland but spent the majority of their careers elsewhere.

"When it came to shortstop, however, I plead guilty. I picked Omar Vizquel, who spent 11 years with the Indians.... I've never enjoyed watching a player more. Game after game, Vizquel did it better, and smoother, than anyone else....

TRIVIA

Going into 2007, Omar Vizquel had 11 Gold Gloves. Who is the only shortstop with more?

Find the answers on pages 159–160.

"The thing I like most about Vizquel is that he never looks like he's working during a game. He's serious when he needs to be, but most of the time he's smiling like a kid playing ball in the backyard with his buddies."

Fans appreciated Vizquel for the same reasons. In addition to his masterful play and all those bare-handed catches, he came across as a really nice, fun-loving guy—which he was. Hoynes recalled a game in Kansas City, where fans were taking part in a limbo contest featuring a digitally enhanced limbo stick on the scoreboard in between innings. When the cameraman focused on Vizquel warming up, the Indians shortstop played along.

Every writer who covered Vizquel with the Indians had their own favorite story. For me, it came early in the 2002 season, when the 5'9", 185-pound Vizquel got off to a hot start with eight home runs by June 10. He was batting .311 with a .513 slugging percentage. I teased him that reporters were going to start asking him about steroids.

VIZQUEL'S BATTING AND FIELDING PERCENTAGES WITH CLEVELAND

Year	Batting	Fielding
1994	.273	.981
1995	.266	.986
1996	.297	.971
1997	.280	.985
1998	.288	.993
1999	.333	.976
2000	.287	.995
2001	.255	.989
2002	.275	.990
2003	.244	.978
2004	.291	.982

"That would be awesome if they asked me about that, a little guy like me," he said, laughing.

The press corps laughed with him. That's usually how it went.

Hoynes, though, had a different story.

"The best thing I ever saw Vizquel do was in 1994 after he made three errors in a game," Hoynes wrote in his series. "The defensive magician had failed in front of his new fans at Jacobs Field.

"Vizquel answered every question from a mob of reporters after the game. Jim Thome, just getting started on being the Indians' all-time home-run leader, had the locker next to Vizquel's. He watched with his eyes and mouth wide open.

"To this day Thome will tell you it's the reason he never ducks a question, good or bad, from the media. Thome figured that if the gold-plated shortstop can do it, so can he."

Vizquel's accountability made him a good teammate, a good role model—and a pretty good author, too. His 2002 autobiography, *Omar!: My Life On and Off the Field* with *Akron Beacon Journal* columnist Bob Dyer, spent four weeks on *The New York Times* Best-Seller List.

Of course, the fact that he called out former teammate Jose Mesa for blowing the save that would have given the Indians a World Series championship over the Florida Marlins in 1997 might have had something to do with that.

It was just another reason fans had to love him. Vizquel, born April 24, 1967, in Caracas, Venezuela, came to the Indians from Seattle in December 1993, for shortstop Felix Fermin, first baseman Reggie Jefferson, and cash. His first season with the Indians was the team's first season at Jacobs Field, and he and the ballpark helped usher in one of the greatest eras in the team's history.

From 1995 to 1999, the team won 471 games and five straight Central Division titles. Twice the Indians advanced to the World Series—in 1995 and 1997. But both times the team and its fans came away disappointed, losing to Atlanta in six games in 1995 and to Florida in seven in 1997. Still, the fans continued to come to the ballpark, and the team sold out a major league record 455 games.

Vizquel, twice honored for his community service, proved to be as accomplished off the field as he was on it with interests in art, music, food, and fashion.

Of course, none of that mattered when it came time to sign a contract extension after the 2004 season. Vizquel was looking for more money than the frugal Indians thought they could spend on a 37-year-old. In addition, the Indians thought they had some promising shortstops in their minor league system.

Three years later, those shortstops hadn't fulfilled that promise. Meanwhile, Vizquel was still going strong, leaving writers like Livingston and Hoynes pining for the good old days.

THE BAD

SNOW DAYS

The snow started falling on Friday and just kept coming. Saturday. Sunday. Monday.

East side, west side, all around the town.

Snow in April in Cleveland is not uncommon. But one to two feet? On Easter Sunday?

From the traditional snow belt on the east side of town to the far western suburbs, everyone was socked in. Easter egg hunts? No chance, unless the kids used a shovel. While there was plenty of grousing, some of the more adaptable residents of the area decided to try and make the best of things. They turned their Christmas lights back on.

Ho. Ho. Ho.

But the Indians were not jolly. For four straight days, from April 6 to 9, 2007, they tried to play baseball games against the Seattle Mariners. For four straight days, they struck out. They scheduled and rescheduled, only to postpone every time.

The optimism that had followed the team from spring training to Chicago, where they took two of three from the White Sox to open the season, was snowed under, replaced by disbelief and more than a little fury—especially after the actual home opener on Friday was delayed four times and then finally called off with the Indians leading, 4–0, with two outs in the top of the fifth—one out away from it counting as a complete game. Indians starter Paul Byrd had not allowed any hits.

"It was one of the most disappointing, grueling days of my career," General Manager Shapiro told reporters. "That being said, I've replayed it a thousand times in my head, and it was the alignment of very unusual and difficult circumstances. I'm not sure, on anyone's part, that things could have been done differently to avoid what was extremely tough and painful....

"The thought was, once we got to...4:45, we had a fairly clear evening. We got lake-effect snow that was not on the radar. Obviously, forecasting weather is a difficult job in Cleveland, Ohio."

Managing a baseball team is no piece of cake, either. A manager has to use whatever means he has at his disposal, and

Snow figures built by Indians fans sit atop the visitor's dugout at Jacobs Field on April 6, 2007, as fans shiver in the background.

former Indians manager Mike Hargrove, now in charge of the Mariners, did just that.

As *Plain Dealer* reporter Paul Hoynes wrote:

They called Mike Hargrove "the Human Rain Delay" when he played because he took so long to get in the batter's box. Now they can call the Seattle manager "the Human Snow Delay."

Hargrove, with his Mariners one strike away from a potential loss to the Indians at Jacobs Field in Friday's home opener, protested that No. 9 hitter Jose Lopez couldn't see Paul Byrd's pitches with two out in the fifth inning because of falling snow and the Indians leading, 4–0.

Plate umpire Alfonzo Marquez, crew chief Rick Reed, Hargrove, and manager Eric Wedge heatedly discussed the matter for several minutes as the snow grew heavier. Seattle had the bases loaded, but all Byrd needed was one more strike to end the inning and make the game official.

Hargrove, arguing that his batters were in danger because they couldn't see the ball, won the debate, and the game was stopped at 7:24 PM for the third time since the first pitch. [The start of the game had been delayed an hour.]

One hour and 17 minutes later, the game was called for good.

Speaking through a pool reporter, Reed said, "We were trying to get the game official if we could. Hargrove's argument was that his hitter could not see and complained to him. He went to home plate to give us his viewpoint, and Eric came out to support his team. Both had legitimate gripes. Was the snow heavier at that point than at any other in the game? It was close."

Byrd was furious with Hargrove and the Mariners.

"When they finally called the game, they were laughing and high-fiving each other in the dugout like they'd gotten away with something," Byrd told reporters. "And they did."

Byrd started the fifth by walking Raul Ibanez, got Richie Sexson on a fly ball, then walked Jose Guillen and Kenji Johjima to load the bases. Yuniesky Betancourt lined out, bringing Lopez to the plate.

"It was snowing as heavy then as when I was walking those guys," Byrd said. "Why didn't Lopez say something right away instead of waiting until I was ahead in the count? I wonder if he would have complained if I was 3–0 on him. Don't wait until it looks like I'm going to get out of the inning to say something."

Naturally, the Indians and their fans were upset. In addition to not winning the game, they lost catcher Victor Martinez for 10 days after he strained a left quadriceps muscle running out a grounder in the third inning. Martinez, the Indians' cleanup hitter, was hitting .500 and leading the team in RBIs when he was injured.

There was a time when the Indians thought that would be the worst thing to come out of the original home opener. They had no idea what was in store for them.

Friday's game was rescheduled as a day-night doubleheader on Saturday. With the weather still threatening, that was postponed and the team scheduled a regular doubleheader on Sunday. That too failed to materialize so another doubleheader was scheduled for Monday. That didn't happen either.

No one had seen anything like it—from a baseball standpoint or a weather standpoint.

"My wife [Amber] and I were standing outside taking pictures of the house, because nobody in California is going to believe us," C.C. Sabathia told reporters.

It took weeks to reschedule the games because it was the Mariners' only trip to Cleveland. The Indians insisted they wanted all four games in Cleveland, but in the end they had to settle for playing three of the games in Cleveland while the other was played in Seattle on September 26.

The Indians tried their best to placate fans, offering tickets to any home game in exchange for the ones that weren't played. Most fans seemed to understand, although one complained to *The Plain Dealer* that it was warmer on the day she bought the tickets in November than on any of the days the Mariners were in town.

Sometime over the lost weekend, with Cleveland still in the grips of the last blast of winter, Indians and baseball officials began to worry about the fate of the next homestand against the Los Angeles Angels. They were due to travel to Cleveland on Monday, April 9, for three games April 10, April 11, and April 12. Officials considered relocating the series to Anaheim, but the Angels did not want to fly cross-country for a game Friday in Boston after hosting a game against Cleveland on Thursday. The Angels wanted a site in the Midwest or East. Domed stadiums in Milwaukee and Houston made them the leading candidates, and when Monday's doubleheader was canceled because the field was still covered by 14 inches of snow, the Indians announced that the Angels series was moving to Milwaukee, which became at least temporarily known as Jacobs Field West.

"This is bizarre, absolutely bizarre," Indians outfielder David Dellucci said as the team packed for the trip. "We might not have many people in the stands, other than workers. You might hear crickets in the rafters."

Dellucci could not have been more wrong. A rowdy crowd of 19,031 took advantage of $10 tickets and had a rip-roaring good time as Sabathia and the Indians, playing for the first time in five days, beat the Angels, 7–6, on April 10.

The Indians did all they could to make themselves feel comfortable. Even though they were the home team, they used the visitor's clubhouse, which they'd used during an interleague series in 2006. Clubhouse manager Tony Amato gave Indians T-shirts to the clubhouse workers. The Indians brought Slider, their mascot, and John Adams, their drummer, to Miller Park. Their computer people e-mailed the players' mug shots, statistics, and graphics to be shown on the scoreboard when they batted. Indians players even heard their favorite music when they stepped into the batter's box.

The Brewers staged their popular sausage race, and Slider and Brewers mascot Bernie Brewer danced the polka.

It was a perfect blend of all the best elements of Milwaukee baseball and Cleveland baseball. In fact, at one point the synergy of the two settings was complete.

When closer Joe Borowski walked out of the bullpen at the start of the ninth inning to protect the Tribe's 7–5 lead, "Wild Thing" played over the loudspeakers. That was Ricky Vaughn's theme song in the movie *Major League*. The movie, about the Indians, was filmed in Milwaukee's old County Stadium.

"I wasn't expecting to hear 'Wild Thing,'" said manager Eric Wedge. "But I should have expected it here.

"There's nothing like playing in front of our fans at Jacobs Field, but these fans were into it. That was nothing short of outstanding. It was a unique situation. I've heard the word 'surreal' a lot today. That's what it felt like. It was just good to get out there and play. To win our first game back was good for us."

The Indians dropped the second game in Milwaukee, 4–1, but found out just how valuable a domed stadium could be. Milwaukee received a record 5.6 inches of snow on April 11. Players, and 16,375 fans who paid $10 apiece again, had to travel through blizzardlike conditions to get to the game—and it was starting to get to them.

After batting practice, Trot Nixon walked into the Indians clubhouse and yelled, "Our next home game will be in Hawaii on Friday."

In the final home game on the road, the Indians beat the Angels, 4–2, before 17,090 fans who took advantage of the final night of $10 baseball.

DID YOU KNOW...

That this was only the second weather-related move for major league games, according to the Society for American Baseball Research and the baseball reference website retrosheet.com? *The Plain Dealer*, citing those references, reported that the first move occurred on September 13–14, 2004, when the Florida Marlins played the Montreal Expos in Chicago's U.S. Cellular Field because of the threat of Hurricane Ivan.

"Milwaukee has been fantastic," said Wedge. "We appreciate the hospitality, but now it's time to get back home and play in front of our fans at Jacobs Field."

So, as luck would have it, the Indians' official home opener was played against the Chicago White Sox on Friday, April 13. Perfect.

As Dennis Manoloff wrote in *The Plain Dealer*, "It took eight days, three opponents, and two venues for the Indians to play their official home opener this season. When the game finally happened, the Indians periodically swung as if still in Milwaukee.

"Their failure to hit enough in the clutch factored heavily in a 6–4 loss to the Chicago White Sox in front of 16,789 at weather-beaten-but-resilient Jacobs Field.

"Ryan Garko's four hits, a career high, and a dominant relief outing by Fernando Cabrera went for naught as the Tribe was 3-for-20 with runners in scoring position and left 13 runners on base."

Wedge fumed. "It was ridiculous," he said.

Of course, that word was as good as any to describe the 2007 season to this point.

For the "opener," it was a balmy 49 degrees, although smart fans wore plenty of down and fleece and brought blankets and sleeping bags, knowing the temperature would plunge as the game wore on.

The pregame ceremonies featured a tribute to the grounds crew, who got a louder ovation than singer Billy Joel, who threw out the first pitch.

And although they finally were able to play at Jacobs Field, the Indians still weren't out of the woods as far as the weather was concerned. The starting time of the second game of the series was changed from 7:05 PM to 1:05 PM. Once again, fans who couldn't make that game were able to exchange their tickets for any other home game.

That Sunday, the Indians took out full-page ads in the *Milwaukee Journal Sentinel* and *The Plain Dealer* thanking fans for the support and understanding. But still the weather would not let up. For the third and final game of the homestand, the team shut down the upper deck at Jacobs Field because of high winds.

Fans who attended that game got a voucher, good for admission to another game during the season.

By the time their off day rolled around on Monday, April 16, the Indians were mentally spent. They lost four of their next five, including three straight at New York. The only good news that week came in the return of Martinez on April 17. He'd suffered a strained left quadriceps muscle running out a grounder on April 6.

"I can't wait until it's 90 or 95 degrees to come back," said Martinez, "or I'd be waiting all year."

Eventually, the team righted itself and won six in a row, climbing to the top of the Central Division. After weeks of haggling, the snowed-out games were rescheduled for May 21, June 11, August 30 in Cleveland, and September 26 in Seattle. The Indians won three of four.

Hargrove was not happy, but no one cared, given that his protest cost the Tribe a chance at winning the original home opener.

"In 10 minutes, I went from being well-liked to being hated," Hargrove said. "I went out and protested the obvious. We couldn't see the ball as hitters. I figured I had one shot at it."

The Indians had some fun with the first makeup game, and not just because they won, 5–2. Fans were greeted with an ice sculpture and fake snow blown by snow machines outside the stadium when they showed up for the game, and the team gave away snow blowers, trips to Winter Haven, Florida, and Peek'n Peak Ski Resort, and auctioned one of the leaf blowers used to clear snow for the home opener. They also gave out 20,000 coupons for a McFlurry ice cream dessert at McDonald's.

The second makeup game wasn't quite as much fun. Byrd, who was one strike away from a victory on April 6, wanted a chance to pay the Mariners back. But he gave up 11 hits and seven runs in four innings as the Indians lost, 8–7. Ibanez hit two two-run home runs to help Seattle build a 7–0 lead.

"I don't know if I was putting too much emphasis on the fact that the Mariners were back in town and I wanted to stick it to them," Byrd said. "Whatever the reason, my ball just didn't have life.... My control just did not show up. This loss is 100 percent on me."

TWO OUTS AWAY

Think Indians fans don't hold a grudge?

In the middle of the 2007 season, when pitcher Jose Mesa came on in relief during a game between the Indians and Philadelphia Phillies in Jacobs Field, Cleveland fans were not glad to see him. Unlike many former players who receive warm welcomes upon their returns, Mesa was booed unmercifully for several minutes when the Phillies called on him.

It had been almost 10 years since Mesa failed to save Game 7 of the 1997 World Series for the Indians against the Florida Marlins, and Indians fans were not going to let him forget it.

It's a bruise that's still sore, a blemish that won't heal.

Losing to the Atlanta Braves in six games of the 1995 World Series was one thing. The Braves pulled out to a 3–1 lead in the Series. Even though the Indians won Game 5 and then lost only 1–0 in Game 6, as a team they weren't going to beat anybody batting .179.

Losing to the Marlins was something else altogether. Although the Marlins won 92 games during the regular season, they still were a wild-card team that was just five years old. The Indians were leading, 2–1, with one out in the bottom of the ninth inning at Pro Player Stadium in Miami when manager Mike Hargrove signaled for Mesa.

Mesa had moved into the bullpen after the 1993 season, when the tragic death of pitcher Steve Olin left the team without a closer. Olin and pitcher Tim Crews were killed in a boating accident during spring training in 1993. Pitcher Bob Ojeda was also severely injured, although he did recover.

DID YOU KNOW...

That Jose Mesa led the Indians with 118 strikeouts and three complete games as a starter in the 1993 season?

Mesa became an All-Star in 1995 and 1996 and was the Rolaids AL Relief Man of the Year in 1995, when he finished second to Seattle's Randy Johnson in the AL Cy Young Award voting and fourth in the MVP voting.

But unlike 1995 and 1996, when he saved 46 and 39 games, respectively, Mesa had just 16 saves in 1997. He had already blown two saves in the postseason. Still, he could get two outs, couldn't he?

Former Indians shortstop Omar Vizquel said he knew it wasn't going to happen. The popular Vizquel wrote his autobiography with *Akron Beacon Journal* writer Bob Dyer in 2002, and he opened the book with that ninth-inning scenario.

The most important asset for a Major League Baseball player is not speed or size or strength. It's mental toughness.

I pride myself on being strong between the ears. At this level of competition, 80 percent of the game is psychological. Unless you have absolute faith in your ability, it doesn't matter how fast you can run or how hard you can throw.

That's why I was worried when I went to the mound in the ninth inning of Game 7 of the 1997 World Series.

Jose Mesa, our ace relief pitcher, had come in to try to protect a one-run lead. All we had to do was get three outs and we'd win the ultimate title. The eyes of the world were focused on every move we made. Unfortunately, Jose's own eyes were vacant. Completely empty. Nobody home. You could almost see right through him.

Jose's first pitch bounced five feet in front of the plate. And, as every Cleveland Indian fan knows, things got worse from there.

Indeed. Moises Alou singled on a 1–1 pitch. Mesa regrouped and struck out Bobby Bonilla and got two strikes on Charles Johnson. Then Johnson singled to right sending Alou to third. Craig Counsell's sacrifice fly to Manny Ramirez in right field tied the game. Mesa retired Jim Eisenreich to end the inning, but the damage was done. Charles Nagy, pitching in relief for the first time in seven seasons, replaced Mesa. With two out in the eleventh inning, Edgar Renteria hit a single to center off Nagy to score Counsell, who'd reached base on an error.

Indians fans waiting to celebrate the team's first World Series championship since 1948 were going to have to wait a little longer.

They'd watched their team win 86 games in the regular season, beat the defending champion New York Yankees (with 96 wins) in the division series and the Baltimore Orioles, winners of 98 regular-season games in the ALCS. They wriggled out of elimination three times in the postseason. They just couldn't do it a fourth time.

"I can't tell you how disappointed I am," Hargrove told reporters after the game. "You only get these chances so many times. But I'm proud of my players. No one gave us a chance to be here.... I wish I had a nickel for every time I heard somebody say that we played in a weak division or called us underachievers. I'm proud of the way we played this year."

Mesa did accept blame for the loss.

"Nagy didn't lose this game, I did," Mesa told reporters afterward. "I get paid to do a job and I didn't do it. It was all my fault."

TRADER LANE

Not everyone hated Frank Lane.

When the former general manager of the Indians died in 1981, Hal Lebovitz, then the sports editor of *The Plain Dealer*, wrote, "I truly liked the man. Even when we argued, I enjoyed being in his commanding presence, covering him, writing about him, and watching him operate.

"Frank Lane was never boring. I'm sorry he won't be coming around anymore."

Not many Indians fans shared Lebovitz's opinion.

"No name invokes such utter, raw hatred among Indians fans as Frank Lane," former *Akron Beacon Journal* columnist Terry Pluto, now of *The Plain Dealer,* wrote in his book *The Curse of Rocky Colavito: A Loving Look at a Thirty-Year Slump.* "If there ever was The Man Who Destroyed the Indians, Lane was it. Fans have suggested hanging, tar-and-feathering, or drawing-and-quartering Frank Lane. But none of that is bad enough.

"For proper punishment, Frank Lane should have been forced to watch every Indians game since 1960."

Well, then. Although it probably seemed a lot longer at the time, Lane was only with the Indians from November 1957 until January 1961. But during that time, he made 50 deals involving 112 players.

It wasn't as if the Indians didn't know what they were getting. The man's nicknames included "Trader Lane" and "Frantic Frank." In seven years with the White Sox, he made 242 trades. He came to Cleveland from St. Louis, where he traded the immensely popular Red Schoendienst and tried to trade the legendary Stan Musial. That was it for him there, although he'd been named Major League Baseball's Executive of the Year by *The Sporting News* in 1957.

When he arrived in Cleveland, the Indians were reeling. They'd finished 88–66 and in second place in 1956 but tumbled to 76–77 and sixth place in 1957, their worst season in 11 years. Star pitcher Herb Score was hit in the eye by a line drive off the bat of Gil McDougald on May 7, and the team never seemed to recover.

Lane didn't waste any time trying to shake things up. Less than a month after he was hired, he made his first trade—sending pitcher Early Wynn and outfielder Al Smith to the Chicago White Sox for outfielder Minnie Minoso and infielder Fred Hatfield.

From that point on, the Indians clubhouse needed a revolving door. Players were always coming and going. Some of the deals were good, some were bad, but there were so many it was hard to tell what might have happened had any of the players stuck around long enough to bond. The Indians' record did improve to 77–76 in 1958 and 89–65 in 1959.

In Pluto's book, former Indians general manager Hank Peters, who also worked in Kansas City and Baltimore, said, "I'm sure that the Indians knew that Lane would keep the team in the newspapers and in the public eye. Fans love trades, and Frank Lane loved to make trades. The bigger the deal, the more controversial, the more he liked it. He made trades just to make them, to keep the pot at the boiling point. There was no off-season with Frank Lane. In the press he was 'Fearless Frank' or 'Trader Lane.' The media loved him, followed him, and wrote about him more than any other general manager. He loved those stories and his reputation for trades. He did make fans pay attention and wonder what he would do next."

Take for instance the end of the 1959 season. With the Indians battling the White Sox for the pennant, manager Joe Gordon told reporters he was going to resign at the end of the season, regardless of the outcome. Lane wanted to beat Gordon to the punch, so he told reporters Gordon would be fired the day the Indians were eliminated. In the meantime, Lane went to court Leo Durocher, former manager of the Brooklyn Dodgers and New York Giants who was working in television. But negotiations with Durocher proved to be difficult, so Lane surprised reporters by announcing that he was offering Gordon a new two-year deal and a $10,000 raise.

If only that had been the end of it. If only Lane had let well enough alone.

But before the Indians even started the 1960 season, Lane made the deal that doomed him in Cleveland: he traded Rocky Colavito.

Colavito was a matinee idol in Cleveland, one of the most popular players to ever play for the Indians. He was a good player with good looks, a clean-living, church-going Catholic who

DID YOU KNOW...

That Frank Lane served as general manager of the National Basketball Association's Chicago Packers and actually refereed football and basketball games before going to work in baseball?

roomed with the popular Score. He hit 21 home runs as a rookie in 1956, when he finished tied with Tito Francona for second place in the Rookie of the Year voting. He hit 25 home runs in 1957 and then broke out in 1958, when he hit 41 home runs and batted .303, finishing third in the MVP voting. He hit 42 homers in 1959, including four in one game.

But some think Lane was jealous of Colavito's popularity. So in the middle of the team's last exhibition game of spring training, apparently with the support of Gordon, Lane sent Colavito to Detroit for Harvey Kuenn, who won the 1959 AL batting title with a .353 average.

"Joe and I believe that the home run is overrated," Lane told reporters. "Look at Washington. They almost led the league in home runs, yet finished last. I don't want to knock Rocky. He is a fine player and a fine man. He may hit 50–55 homers in Detroit. But we've given up 40 homers for 40 doubles. We've added 50 singles and taken away 50 strikeouts.... I'll probably make bobby-soxers mad at me, but they've been mad at me before.... I realize that Colavito is very popular. There were many people who came to the park to see him hit a home run, whereas they wouldn't come to the park just to see Kuenn hit a single. But those singles and doubles win just as many games as home runs.... Rocky's best year was 1958 when he batted over .300 and hit 41 homers, but our attendance was only 650,000 because we didn't have a contending club."

With Indians fans still reeling over the loss of Colavito, Lane sent Score to the White Sox the next day.

Did those deals lead to the demise of the Indians that season? At one point, things were going so bad that Lane was rumored to have threatened to trade his whole team for the Tigers. When that didn't work, he settled for trading Gordon to Detroit for manager Jimmie Dykes. (According to Pluto's book, the managers actually could not be traded but had to be fired by their respective clubs and rehired by the other club.)

The Indians finished 1960 with a 76–78 record. Lane was gone, but before he left he sent Kuenn to the San Francisco Giants.

In spite of his controversial stay in Cleveland, Lane went on to work as an executive with the Kansas City Athletics, Baltimore Orioles, and Milwaukee Brewers before finishing his career as a scout for the California Angels and Texas Rangers.

He died in a Dallas nursing home at 85 years of age. According to Pluto's book, only eight people attended his funeral.

THE UGLY

A BLACK EYE FOR THE FRANCHISE

When the Indians first introduced the notion of 10¢ Beer Nights early in the 1970s, longtime Cleveland sportswriter Dan Coughlin thought the idea was charming.

He recalled the first one fondly, with a Dixieland band strolling the grounds, evoking a gentler era in the early days of the game.

"It was so innocent," said Coughlin, now a popular Cleveland sportscaster who still does some writing.

No one used the word *innocent* to describe what happened at Cleveland Municipal Stadium on the night of June 4, 1974. Instead, words like *riot*, *melee*, and *zoo* were used in the wake of a disgusting debacle on Beer Night.

Coughlin was even punched in the jaw—twice—while trying to interview some of the rowdy youths, who, fueled by 10¢ cups of beer, stormed the field and forced the umpires to call the game and declare the Texas Rangers, 9–0, winners by forfeit. Coughlin was enjoying a busman's holiday, watching the game on his night off, but volunteered for duty when the trouble broke out. Asked if it was the wildest thing he'd covered in his decades-long career, Coughlin said, "Without a doubt."

The front page of *The Plain Dealer* the next day carried the headline "Stadium beer night fans riot, ending Indians' rally in forfeit" and detailed the chilling developments of what Russell

Schneider referred to as "one of the ugliest incidents in the history of the Cleveland baseball club," in *The Cleveland Indians Encyclopedia.*

"That's probably the closest we'll come to seeing someone getting killed in the game of baseball," Texas manager Billy Martin

Umpire Joe Brinkman holds a fan who was injured during the Beer Night melee at Cleveland Stadium on June 4, 1974. The Indians forfeited the game to the Texas Rangers after fans, fueled by 10¢ beers, stormed the field in the ninth inning.

told reporters. "In the 25 years I've played, I've never seen any crowd act like that. It was ridiculous."

Umpire Nestor Chylak's right hand was cut and bleeding after being hit by a chair thrown from the stands as he made his way from the field with the other umpires.

"They were uncontrolled beasts," Chylak said of the hooligans. "I've never seen anything like it except in a zoo."

Some think the genesis of the incident was in Texas a week earlier, when a fight broke out between the Rangers and Indians during a game. Rangers fans threw beer at the Indians and wanted to fight, too. But, in fact, the two teams helped each other get out of harm's way during the incident in Cleveland.

"Billy called to thank us for helping him and his players," Indians manager Ken Aspromonte said. "I've never seen anything like that in all my life and I have played baseball all over the world.... Billy feels as badly as we do, but he was grateful we helped."

The stage was set for trouble almost from the start, when more than 25,000 fans showed up for the game, more than double the crowd expected. Although there were more policemen than usual at the game, there were not nearly enough to handle that kind of crowd.

According to *The Plain Dealer*, fans started racing across the outfield in the fourth inning and one even stopped and undressed in the sixth inning. Fans also threw cups, bottles, and firecrackers onto the field, and when some of the fireworks landed near the Rangers bullpen, the pitchers returned to the dugout in the seventh inning. The Indians pitchers followed not long after.

The Rangers held a 5–3 lead going into the bottom of the ninth inning, but with one out, Ed Crosby hit a run-scoring single to make it 5–4. John Lowenstein's sacrifice fly scored Crosby to tie the score. That would be the last official play of the game.

A couple of fans jumped onto the field and tried to steal the cap of Rangers right fielder Jeff Burroughs.

"I could see that there was sort of a riot psychology," said Burroughs, who jammed his left thumb. "You have to realize all I had to protect myself with was my fists."

SOUND FAMILIAR?

Twenty-seven years after the Beer Night debacle at Cleveland Municipal Stadium, there was a similarly ugly incident at the new Cleveland Browns stadium that stood virtually on the same spot.

Jacksonville led Cleveland, 15–10, with 48 seconds left of the NFL game on December 16, 2001. Officials used instant replay to overturn a catch by Quincy Morgan at the Jacksonville 9-yard line. The Browns had already run another play, which usually means the preceding play cannot be reviewed, but officials said they had received an electronic signal from the replay official before the play and simply failed to stop game in time.

When the catch was overruled, giving the ball to Jacksonville, angry fans pelted the field with plastic bottles, some of which still contained beer or water. Officials, fearing for their safety and that of the players and coaches, first ruled the game over. But under orders from NFL commissioner Paul Tagliabue, the game resumed 25 minutes later. Jacksonville quarterback Mark Brunell took a knee twice against a mishmash Browns defensive unit that actually included three offensive players since most of their teammates already had undressed and showered.

As badly as the fans behaved, what some found most offensive was the reaction from Browns officials who refused to criticize the unruly fans after the game. Said Browns president Carmen Policy to reporters after the game, "Cleveland is not going to take a black eye. Our fans had their hearts ripped out.... I like the fact that our fans cared.... The bottles are plastic. They don't carry much of a wallop." Owner Al Lerner told reporters, "Everybody controlled themselves considering they had spent 60 minutes outside in cold weather.... It wasn't pleasant. I'm not going to suggest anything like that. But it wasn't World War III." It must be noted it was 44 degrees at kickoff, balmy weather in Cleveland in December.

Burroughs fought back as Rangers and Indians streamed to his defense.

"Burroughs seemed to be surrounded," Martin said. "Maybe it was silly for us to go out there but we weren't about to leave a man out there on the field unprotected. It seemed that he might be destroyed. They would have killed him. I guess these fans just can't handle good beer. There were knives out there, too. We're fortunate somebody didn't get stabbed."

The players were quickly outnumbered by the scores of fans, many of them drunk, who poured onto the field. The police called for reinforcements and at least 11 people eventually were arrested. But that was not much comfort as the frightened players fought their way to safety. Many suffered cuts and bruises. Pitcher Tom Hilgendorf was hit on the head and shoulders with a steel folding chair thrown from the stands. Ranger pitcher Steve Foucault and pitching coach Art Fowler were each punched in the eye. Fowler also injured his left elbow when he fell down the steps to the dugout running off the field.

It probably took about 10 minutes for the players to safely reach their clubhouses; the fighting lasted about 20 more minutes after the players departed. Chylak instructed the public address announcer to wait until the players and umpires were off the field before announcing that the game had been forfeited.

"This was a mean, ugly, frightening crowd," Indians pitcher Dick Bosman said.

"Those people were like animals," a stunned Aspromonte said. "But it's not just baseball. It's the society we live in. Nobody seems to care about anything. We complained about their people in Arlington last week when they threw beer on us and taunted us to fight. But look at our people. They were worse. I don't know what it was, and I don't know who's to blame, but I'm scared."

OTHER FORFEITS IN INDIANS HISTORY

Wins

July 23, 1901, vs. Washington
July 20, 1918, vs. Philadelphia
April 26, 1925, vs. Chicago

Losses

August 8, 1903, vs. Detroit
September 9, 1917, vs. Chicago

Immediately after the incident, American League president Leland S. MacPhail Jr. said he would ban Beer Nights in Cleveland Municipal Stadium—although he later relented.

"We expected trouble there because of the fight last week in Texas," MacPhail told *The Plain Dealer* in a telephone interview after the game. "The problem tonight was not the players. It was the fans. It was an unfortunate timing for the Beer Night promotion. I talked to officials of the Indians and the Rangers before the game and [general manager] Phil Seghi of the Indians told me they had doubled security forces for Beer Night. It's an unfortunate situation but the Indians lost the ballgame and that's the penalty they have to pay."

The Indians officially protested the forfeit the next day.

"While we deplore the incidents which led to the forfeiture, we also feel that there was no warning given to the fans during the course of the game by the umpires that any continuation of interruptions of play would lead to a declaration of a forfeiture of the game," Seghi wrote to MacPhail in a telegram. But he admitted he knew the forfeit would stand.

Meanwhile, baseball officials around the country were outraged. Brewers owner Bud Selig, who would become commissioner, called the incident "unbelievable" and "disgusting." He set a two-beer limit for the Brewers Beer Night that was scheduled later that month.

AN ANGRY MAN

Where to start with Albert Belle?

His talent was undeniable; his behavior unconscionable. There is a long, long list of his abusive outbursts toward reporters, fans, even team officials. Unfortunately, his problems did not end after a degenerative hip problem forced his early retirement in 2000. In 2006, Belle was jailed in Arizona after being charged with stalking a woman with whom he'd had a five-year relationship.

His troubles started before he joined the Indians. Belle and his twin brother, Terry, were born on August 25, 1966, in Shreveport,

Louisiana. Their father was a high school coach. Their mother was a math teacher. Albert Belle, who went by the name of Joey until early in his major league career, was a two-time all-state baseball player at Huntington High School, where he also played football and was a member of the National Honor Society. When he moved on to Louisiana State University, he was a first-team All-Southeastern Conference selection in 1986 and 1987, when he had a combined .332 batting average and .670 slugging average with 49 home runs and 172 RBIs. In 1986, he was involved in a confrontation with a fan in the stands who allegedly made racist remarks, and Belle was suspended from the College World Series. Still, the Indians drafted him in the second round of the 1987 draft and two years later he was in the major leagues. By 1993, he made the first of five straight All-Star appearances.

But he'd already exhibited the temper that overshadowed his talent.

Longtime Indians beat writer Jim Ingraham of the *News-Herald* recalled an incident in 1991 at Cleveland Municipal Stadium, where Belle threw a baseball at a fan in the stands who was heckling Belle about his alcohol abuse and rehabilitation.

"That was the first inkling we had that his reputation was justified," Ingraham said. "The guy was heckling him from left field in the old stadium. He threw a line drive that hit the guy in the chest. This was in the days before ESPN, so there was no replay of it. It was like, 'Did I just see what I thought I just saw?' We'd heard about his problems in the minor leagues and college, but this was the first tangible evidence this guy was going to be a problem for the team."

The evidence mounted—inside and outside the clubhouse.

Manager Mike Hargrove told a story about challenging Belle after a lackadaisical catch and throw cost the Indians a game. Hargrove told coach Jeff Newman that he was leaving the door to his office open and if it got quiet, Newman should come in and rescue him.

"I said things to him I've never said to any other man," Hargrove told *The Plain Dealer*'s Bob Dolgan for a newspaper article that became part of Dolgan's book, *Heroes, Scamps and Good*

Guys: 101 Colorful Characters from Cleveland Sports History. "He reacted like he knew he was wrong. I think that was the turning point in our relationship."

Not everyone was so lucky. Reporters told stories of Belle ripping a tape he didn't like out of the tape recorder in the team's clubhouse and firing it against the wall, where it exploded. He liked it cold in the clubhouse, and in the old stadium, he'd come in between innings and turn down the thermostat. Teammates or team employees would turn it up when he left. But the new Jacobs Field had an automatic thermostat. No problem. When it wasn't cold enough, Belle used his bat to smash it off the wall, leading teammates to call him "Mr. Freeze" and make the No. 8 above his locker into a snowman.

Plain Dealer columnist Bud Shaw tells the following story:

I walked into Jacobs Field one day and heard the words no reporter ever wants to hear—'Albert is looking for you.' Seems he took offense to a largely flattering column about the fact that he had become such a student of hitting. Manager Mike Hargrove and coach Davey Nelson had both told me that Belle kept an exhaustive account of each at-bat on index cards and that he would come up between at-bats to write down the situation, the count, the umpire, what each pitcher threw him, etc. Albert accused me of going through his locker, convinced that was the only way I would know about his index cards. Clearly I had not been anywhere near his locker. No one with a choice in the matter ever went near him or his locker. Obviously, he hadn't read the column. It was totally irrational and so totally Albert. A confrontation followed in which he called me the kind of names heard in the Bada Bing Lounge when somebody questions Tony Soprano's authority. Sandy Alomar broke it up just as I was about to hit Albert's fist with my face.

I asked for a meeting with general manager John Hart, in which I told him he was going to have a serious problem one day if Belle's behavior wasn't addressed with him. I remember pointing out to John that the team would soon be in the postseason surrounded by national media, including women, and that Belle stood a real chance of embarrassing the organization. John listened, apologized for Belle's antics, and told me he'd like to assure me that talking to Albert would do some good. But, Hart said, he had his doubts given that Albert had previously cursed both owner Dick Jacobs (during negotiations) and American League president Dr. Bobby Brown (after a suspension and while being greeted by Brown at an All-Star Game). It didn't make me feel any better that he had mistreated the AL president and the guy who paid his salary, but I understood I shouldn't wait for an apology from Belle.

In 1995, Belle used his Ford Explorer to chase down some teenage trick-or-treaters who threw eggs at his condominium in Euclid, slightly bumping one of them with his SUV in the process. The teen later sued, but the case was settled out of court and the record sealed. In 1996, he threw a baseball at a photographer. In 1997, Belle admitted losing at least $40,000 in bets placed on professional and college football and basketball games, but not on Major League Baseball.

Most of the incidents didn't make much news outside of Cleveland. But there were others that became embarrassing national stories.

In 1994, when his batting average soared to .357, the Chicago White Sox accused Belle of corking his bat during a game on July 15. The charge proved to be true and netted a 10-game suspension (later reduced to seven) in spite of the fact that teammate Jason Grimsley made a heroic, some might say idiotic, attempt to clear Belle. The 6'3", 180-pound Grimsley, whose own baseball career came to a dramatic end in 2006 when he was found with a supply of human growth hormone while pitching for the Arizona Diamondbacks and left the team, climbed up through the ceiling tiles in Hargrove's office in Comiskey Park, wriggled through the air ducts to the umpire's room, climbed down, and replaced the confiscated corked bat with one of Paul Sorrento's bats that was uncorked. (Apparently it was impossible to replace one Belle bat with another because all of them were corked.) Although Grimsley was never caught (he revealed his part in the caper in a 1999 article in *The New York Times*), the umpires discovered the obvious switch because the player's names are printed on their bats. They demanded a return of the original bat, which led to the suspension.

That incident seemed just plain silly in comparison to the low point that occurred during the 1995 World Series, when Belle verbally lambasted former NBC broadcaster Hannah Storm in the Indians dugout two hours before the start of Game 3. Storm was in the dugout to conduct a pre-arranged interview with Kenny Lofton of the Indians. Despite the verbal assault by Belle, she stood her ground, conducted the interview, and then filed a complaint with Major League Baseball. MLB eventually fined Belle $50,000 for the incident, which cast a pall over the Indians' return to the World Series for the first time in 41 years.

INDIANS WHO LED THE AMERICAN LEAGUE IN HOME RUNS

Bobby Roth, 1915, 7
Al Rosen, 1950, 37
Larry Doby, 1952, 32
Al Rosen, 1953, 43
Larry Doby 1954, 32
Rocky Colavito, 1959, 42
　(tied with Harmon Killebrew)
Albert Belle, 1995, 50

"That 1995 season should have been a celebration, but it wasn't because of him," Paul Hoynes, the longtime baseball writer for *The Plain Dealer,* said, referring to Belle. "He was like Darth Vader."

With his sport still trying to recover from a labor dispute that shortened the 1994 season, commissioner Bud Selig thought the outburst was costly.

"It's a very sensitive period for baseball," Selig told reporters. "We have to be reaching out to people. We need to have closer synergy with the fans and players and clubs. It's extremely disappointing."

John Hart, the Indians' general manager at the time, said he could put up with Belle's antics because he produced during games.

"I loved him from 7:00 to 10:00 PM," Hart told *The Plain Dealer*'s Dolgan. "But he could suck all the joy out of a franchise."

Of the incident with Storm, Hart said, "We had a great team. We had the eyes of the world on us. We should have been a feel-good story, but we weren't because of Albert."

Eventually, Hart had seen and heard enough.

"Fans would call complaining that he cursed their son. It went on and on. Trouble made him tick.... He was a fine player, but he never enjoyed his great fortune. It still bothers me to think a man so gifted could be so miserable."

Of covering Belle during his years with the Indians, Hoynes said, "It was a circus. It got to be Albert Belle and the Indians, not just the Indians. Every time we were in New York, we wound up waiting outside the American League president's office because Albert was always getting suspended for something. He made your life miserable. You never knew what he was going to do."

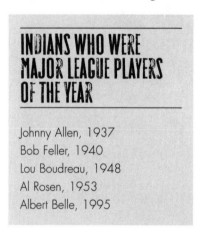

INDIANS WHO WERE MAJOR LEAGUE PLAYERS OF THE YEAR

Johnny Allen, 1937
Bob Feller, 1940
Lou Boudreau, 1948
Al Rosen, 1953
Albert Belle, 1995

Stories like these no doubt are at least part of the reason Belle likely will never receive all the accolades he deserved. In 1995, for example, he led the American League in runs, home runs, slugging percentage, and total bases and shared the RBI lead with Boston's Mo Vaughn. Yet the popular Vaughn was named MVP that season as some voters just couldn't bring themselves to elect the surly Belle, who generally ignored reporters when he wasn't abusive toward them. Many of those same reporters also vote for the Hall of Fame, and Belle's chances of being elected are iffy at best, in spite of his great talent on the field.

After the 1996 season, Belle signed a $55 million free-agent contract with the Chicago White Sox. Upon his first return to

Jacobs Field, fans showered him with fake paper money. He responded with a three-run home run and an obscene gesture for which he was fined. In 1999, he signed a free-agent deal with the Baltimore Orioles, but the hip injury ended his career in 2000.

BIG LOSERS

On September 15, 1901, in their first season of existence as the franchise that would become today's Indians, the Cleveland Blues lost to the host Detroit Tigers, 21–0. It would take more than 100 years for the Indians to lose a game by that large a margin again.

On June 4, 2002, the Indians lost at Minnesota, 23–2, to tie the record for largest margin of defeat set all those years ago.

In a discussion of that loss to the Twins, coupled with an earlier 21–2 loss to the California Angels that season, *Plain Dealer* sportswriter Hoynes wrote, "It's not the kind of history that will sell tickets, but it may attract an ambulance chaser or two if they're involved in another train wreck of a game."

At some point, a reporter covering that kind of game just runs out of things to say. Apparently things were easier back in 1901, when one long paragraph, with a Detroit dateline and no byline, sufficed in describing pitcher Jack Bracken's worst day. The writer—and the team—got a break that day when umpires called the game.

Detroit closed the season in this city today in a blaze of glory. They batted young Bracken for twenty-three hits with a total of thirty-five bases and beat the Cleveland Indians by the one-sided score of 21 to 0, the game being called in the visitor's half of the eighth, to prevent Detroit from scoring more runs. Bracken wanted to quit in the middle of the sixth inning, but Capt. LaChance made him take his medicine and stick until the umpire finally relieved him by calling the game. There was only one inning in which Detroit did not score and every man on the team got at least one hit. Dillon led with four, but McAllister had the best total, making a home run and two doubles. Bracken had few excuses, though three errors were made behind him. Siever pitched grand ball for the home team, holding his opponents down to five scattered singles. Elberfeld quit the game in the sixth, Shaw going to show and Buelow behind the bat. The Detroit outfielders made some splendid catches. Holmes, in the fifth, captured a short fly over second after a very hard run. Barrett pulled down a long drive from Beck's bat in the fourth and the same player was robbed of another hit in the sixth, when Nance stopped his hot drive with his gloved hand and recovered the ball before it dropped to the ground. Pickering also made a nice catch for the visitors. The least said about the Detroit scoring the better.

Hoynes had to come up with a considerably longer story and a notebook, including quotes (and first names). And, since his game wasn't at the end of the season, he had to rehash it all again the next day. Of course, that led to a hilarious tidbit about relief pitcher Mark Wohlers, who gave up five runs in a third of an inning in the 23–2 loss. Apparently security officials wouldn't let Wohlers in before the game because he didn't have the right credentials. The next night, he told reporters he had no problem getting in. "They rolled out the red carpet and had a golf cart waiting for me," he said.

In addition, manager Charlie Manuel, a great storyteller, regaled reporters with a tale about managing Triple A in Portland, where his team blew a 9–0 lead with two outs in the ninth inning.

"Our right fielder dropped three straight fly balls and our left fielder misplayed one with the bases loaded," Manuel said. "I saw things in Portland that I never want to see again."

Manuel probably wasn't too crazy about what he saw in Minnesota either.

"We just got the hell beat out of us," Manuel said after the game. "When something like that happens, all you can do is watch. There sure isn't a whole lot of managing involved. They just teed off on us."

Mark Wohlers wipes sweat from his face after being replaced on the mound in the seventh inning of the Indians' 23–2 loss to the Minnesota Twins on June 4, 2002. Wohlers pitched one out in the inning while the Twins scored 10 runs.

The Twins set a club record with 25 hits and tied an American League record with four players with four hits each—Jacque Jones, Dustan Mohr, A.J. Pierzynski, and Luis Rivas. Mohr, Pierzynski, and Rivas made up the bottom of the Twins' batting order. Sadly, it was the fourth time the Indians allowed that many hits, albeit the first time in 66 years.

Ryan Drese started the game and left with the bases loaded and no outs in the fourth inning. The Twins led, 3–1, at the time.

"He couldn't throw a strike," Manuel said. "He was all over the place."

Chad Paronto replaced him and got out of the jam almost unscathed. He allowed two runs to score, and the second one

THE CRYBABIES

It seems like such a silly insult now, a ridiculous thing to call a team of grown men. But the 1940 Indians were called the "Crybabies" for their revolt against manager Oscar Vitt.

Outwardly, it looked as if the team was having a great year. Bob Feller opened the season with a no-hitter in Chicago. The Indians finished 89–65 and were in first place for 73 days. They fell as low as third, but for only seven days. But apparently Vitt's grating personality wore on the players, who accused him of criticizing them behind their backs and in the newspapers and undermining their confidence.

According to author Russell Schneider in *The Cleveland Indians Encyclopedia*, after the Indians slipped to third place in June, well-respected pitcher Mel Harder went to owner Alva Bradley and told him, "We think we've got a good chance to win the pennant, but we'll never win it with Vitt as manager. If we can get rid of him, we can win. We all feel sure of that."

Bradley balked and when the story hit the papers, the players either agreed or were ordered to sign a statement taking back their criticism of the manager, although only 21 players actually did so. About a month after the Tigers beat the Indians to win the pennant with three days left in the season, Bradley wound up firing Vitt, who had a 262–198–2 record in three seasons. He was replaced by Roger Peckinpaugh in 1941.

came in only because he forgot to step on first base to complete a double play.

So the Twins took a 5–1 lead into the fifth inning. Paronto gave up a two-run home run to Mohr and a run-scoring double to Jones as the Twins pushed their lead to 8–1. Charles Nagy relieved Paronto and gave up another run to make it 9–1 after five.

Then the roof fell in—figuratively speaking, of course, since the only actual disaster in the Metrodome took place in the Indians' bullpen. The Twins added four runs in the sixth off Nagy. He faced five batters in the seventh and they all scored en route to a 10-run inning for Minnesota. In all, the usually dependable

Nagy allowed nine runs on eight hits in two innings. He was replaced by Wohlers, who gave up a two-run single to Rivas and a three-run home run to Jones.

By the time Ricardo Rincon relieved Wohlers and managed to get the last two outs of the seventh and all three in the eighth, it hardly mattered.

The Indians got no sympathy from their manager—or the Twins.

"You never feel sorry for the other team in a situation like that," Pierzynski said. "You might feel sorry for the pitchers because they're getting knocked around. But that means your teammates are getting hits. In that situation, you just don't try to show anybody up."

IN THE CLUTCH

SAVING GRACE

It was all so familiar to Indians fans.

With one out in the ninth inning, Bob Wickman gave up a single, and the runner went to second on a walk. Wickman struck out the next batter, then walked the following batter before getting another strikeout to end the game and earn his 12th save of the year.

Standard operating procedure.

Only this time, Wickman was pitching for the Atlanta Braves against the Indians during an interleague game in Jacobs Field in the middle of the 2007 season. Wickman was traded to Atlanta on July 20, 2006, two months after becoming the Indians' all-time leader in saves and almost six years to the day after he was acquired from the Milwaukee Brewers.

Not every one of his 139 saves with the Indians was a roller-coaster ride. It only seemed that way.

When Wickman became the Indians' leader on May 7, 2006, in Seattle, Paul Hoynes wrote in *The Plain Dealer:*

> It wouldn't have been a save worth remembering if it had been easy.
>
> Bob Wickman went into the Indians' record book as their top closer the way he should have—on a tightrope over the shark tank with a hard wind blowing.

Wickman passed Doug Jones as the Tribe's all-time saves leader with 130 in Sunday's 2–0 victory over Seattle at Safeco Field. He started the ninth after eight shutout innings by C.C. Sabathia and retired cleanup hitter Richie Sexson on a grounder.

Then the fins started flashing and the wind started blowing.

Carl Everett singled to right field and Adrian Beltre singled to center to put runners on first and second. Kenji Johjima was next and Wickman—he'd never faced the Japanese catcher, but had studied him extensively—

Bob Wickman pitches to the Rangers' Hank Blaylock on April 28, 2006. In the game, Wickman tied a career high with his 21st consecutive save and matched Doug Jones for the Cleveland club record with 129.

threw three straight fastballs. Johjima sent number three to shortstop Jhonny Peralta, who started a game-ending 6–4–3 double play.

"It was typical Wicky fashion," said Sabathia. "I told someone in here, I don't even get nervous anymore. I knew he'd get that ground ball. I'm just glad I could be part of it."

After Wickman broke that Indians' record for saves, Bob Dolgan examined Wickman's record in his popular "Glad You Asked" feature in *The Plain Dealer*. Dolgan found that Wickman had 40 1–2–3 innings among his 130 saves for the Indians. He was also perfect on three other occasions, when he came in to get the final out or final two outs. He missed three other times because of an error by one of his fielders. In 2000, his first year with Cleveland, Wickman got the side out in 7 of his 14 saves. In 2001, he was 10-of-32. In 2002, he was 6-of-20 before getting elbow surgery. In 2004, he was 5-of-13. In 2005, he was 14-of-45. In 2006, he had one perfect inning among his first six saves. He has put at least two men on in 34 saves.

WICKMAN WITH THE INDIANS

139 saves
17 blown saves
255 games
8 wins
16 losses
3.23 ERA

Oddly enough, in his first three games with Atlanta, the former Indians closer was near perfect in three innings. No runs, one hit allowed, two saves. What was even more surprising was that the 38-year-old Wickman, who had talked of retiring after the 2006 season, not only returned to the Braves in 2007 but talked of continuing to pitch. His likely retirement played a part in the Indians' willingness to trade him.

"A year ago at this time, my hip was a little sore and stuff like that," Wickman told reporters upon his return to Cleveland with the Braves. "I didn't really think my body would come around the way it did the second half of last season and this season, so far.... It would be cool to get to 300 saves. If I'm put in a situation where I don't believe I could be put into the closer's role or can't compete in the closer's role, then I'll quit this year. But if I still feel I can compete in the closer's role and somebody's willing to give me a job for that, I'll definitely try again."

No one could complain about the job Wickman did while he was with the Indians. He was a creature of habit. A Wisconsin native who attended the University of Wisconsin–Whitewater, he wore a Green Bay Packers T-shirt under his baseball uniform. Upon arriving in the bullpen he shook everyone's hands and then hugged the bullpen coach. Even if he wasn't being used, he threw in the bullpen every four or five days to stay loose. He said he needed only 15 or 16 pitches to warm up.

INDIANS SAVES LEADERS

Bob Wickman 139
Doug Jones 129
Jose Mesa 104
Mike Jackson 94
Ray Narleski 53
Steve Olin 48
Jim Kern 46
Sid Monge 46
Gary Bell 45
Joe Borowski 45
Ernie Camacho 44

"Some guys say they don't turn it on until they get into a game," he once told *The Plain Dealer*. "I don't take anything for granted when I'm throwing in the bullpen. I throw at 100 percent. To me, my bullpens are just like games."

He also admitted it hurt when he was traded by the Brewers to the Indians in 2000, along with Steve Woodard and Jason Bere for Richie Sexson, Paul Rigdon, and Kane Davis.

"I had four great years with the Brewers," said Wickman, who grew up in Green Bay. "It was wonderful..... Leaving the Brewers organization is not what hurt. Baseball is a business and everyone knows that. What hurt is having to leave the family members I had in the area. The deal did not really come as a big surprise. It had been talked about for a week or so, and they finally pulled the trigger."

Wickman became the Indians' closer immediately, replacing Steve Karsay.

BOB WICKMAN CAREER STATISTICS

Year	Team	W	L	ERA	G	GS	CG	SHO	SV	SVO	IP	H	R	ER	HR	HBP	BB	SO
1992	New York Yankees	6	1	4.11	8	8	0	0	—	—	50.1	51	25	23	2	2	20	21
1993	New York Yankees	14	4	4.63	41	19	1	0	4	—	140.0	156	82	72	13	5	69	70
1994	New York Yankees	5	4	3.09	53	0	0	0	6	—	70.0	54	26	24	3	1	27	56
1995	New York Yankees	2	4	4.05	63	1	0	0	1	—	80.0	77	38	36	6	5	33	51
1996	Milwaukee Brewers	3	0	3.24	12	0	0	0	0	—	16.2	12	9	6	0	0	10	14
1996	New York Yankees	4	1	4.67	58	0	0	0	0	—	79.0	94	41	41	5	5	34	61
1997	Milwaukee Brewers	7	6	2.73	74	0	0	0	1	—	95.2	89	32	29	8	3	41	78
1998	Milwaukee Brewers	6	9	3.72	72	0	0	0	25	—	82.1	79	38	34	6	5	38	71
1999	Milwaukee Brewers	3	8	3.39	71	0	0	0	37	45	74.1	75	31	28	5	4	39	60
2000	Milwaukee Brewers	1	3	3.38	26	0	0	0	14	17	26.2	27	12	10	0	2	11	11
2000	Cleveland Indians	2	2	2.93	43	0	0	0	16	20	46.0	37	18	15	0	0	20	44
2001	Cleveland Indians	5	0	2.39	70	0	0	0	32	35	67.2	61	18	18	2	2	26	66
2002	Cleveland Indians	1	3	4.46	36	0	0	0	20	22	34.1	42	22	17	3	1	36	36
2004	Cleveland Indians	0	2	4.25	30	0	0	0	13	14	29.2	33	17	14	5	2	10	10
2005	Cleveland Indians	0	4	2.47	64	0	0	0	45	50	62.0	57	17	17	4	1	21	26
2006	Cleveland Indians	0	2	1.04	28	0	0	0	18	19	26.0	24	7	3	1	0	11	25
2006	Atlanta Braves	0	4	4.18	29	0	0	0	15	18	28.0	29	15	13	1	1	17	17
2007	Cleveland Indians	3	3	3.92	49	0	0	0	20	26	43.2	48	22	19	4	2	20	41
2007	Atlanta Braves	1	1	1.35	8	0	0	0	0	—	6.2	6	2	1	2	0	2	6
2007	Arizona Diamondbacks	0	1	—	0	0	0	0	0	—	0.0	0	1	0	0	0	0	0
Totals		63	61	3.57	835	28	1	0	267	—	1059.0	1051	469	420	80	38	432	785

"He's most effective when he's pitching one inning," Indians manager Charlie Manuel said. "Steve Karsay and Paul Shuey can go more than one inning."

After six productive seasons in Cleveland, Wickman was not nearly as upset when he was sent to Atlanta on July 20, 2006.

"I liked the idea of going to Atlanta," he said. "When I was a free agent the last two years, I was either going to come here [Atlanta] or stay in Cleveland."

GRACE UNDER PRESSURE

There are few reminders of his baseball career in the office of Andre Thornton.

Thornton, the former Indians star, is now CEO and chairman of ASW Global, a supply-chain management company in Mogadore, Ohio, just outside Akron. The company provides public distribution and warehousing services for the polymer, metalworking, electronics, and retail support industries.

There is one black-and-white sketch of him and another of the Indians' Big Four—pitchers Bob Feller, Early Wynn, Bob Lemon, and Mike Garcia—along with manager Al Lopez. There is a framed, signed letter from then-commissioner Peter Ueberroth upon Thornton's retirement in 1987.

Other than that, the office could belong to any other business executive. Two windows light up the white walls, which are filled with photos and mementoes from Thornton's many other civic activities. There's a large desk and chair with a computer on a table behind them, a round table with four chairs, and a credenza full of books. From one shelf, he pulls out a slim paperback, *Triumph Born of Tragedy: The Story of Romance and Courage in the Life of Andre Thornton*, as told to Al Janssen. He opens the front cover and, with a practiced hand, writes on the title page, "I pray this book will be a blessing."

The story is his own and tells how he overcame the tragic loss of his beloved wife, Gert, and two-year-old daughter, Theresa, in a car accident on an icy Pennsylvania road shortly after his first season with the Indians in 1977. Thornton and his four-year-old son, Andre Thornton Jr., survived. It tells of Thornton's great faith and how that faith not only helped form the foundation of his family life, but how it helped heal the wounds when that family was shattered in the accident and made him stronger as he pressed on in his career as he formed a new family.

Much like his office, the baseball references in the book are few and far between, used mainly as a vehicle to explain how his faith grew and got him through difficult circumstances. It is touchingly candid, achingly honest. After reading it, it is clear how much he loved his wife and daughter and how, for him, life has been about much more than his baseball career. In fact, it helps explain a comment he made when asked why he had so few baseball souvenirs on display. "I'm not one who lingers in the past," he said.

Yet he was gracious enough to indulge reporters for at least one week in the middle of August 2007, when the Indians named him to their Hall of Fame during induction ceremonies in Jacobs Field. The weather was beautiful, the Indians were playing the rival New York Yankees, and the ballpark was sold out for the ceremony, all of which brought back good memories for Thornton. He played with the Indians for 10 years, from 1977–87, on some bad teams in front of lots of empty seats at the drafty old Cleveland Municipal Stadium.

TRIVIA

Who gave up Duane Kuiper's only home run?

Find the answers on pages 159–160.

But there were good times too, and Thornton was responsible for many of them. He remains the team's career leader as a designated hitter with 125 home runs and 459 RBIs, and his 214 total home runs rank seventh on the team's all-time list. In 1982, Thornton had a huge season with 32 home runs and 116 RBIs while batting .273. He walked 109 times, becoming only the second Indian to register 100 walks and 100 RBIs in the same season. After a knee injury that caused him to miss the 1980 season and limited him to 69 games in 1981, he was named the Comeback Player of the Year in 1982, as well as an All-Star and the Indians' Man of the Year

TRIPLE PLAYS

It was probably more quirky than clutch, but Duane Kuiper hit two bases-loaded triples in a 17–5 victory at New York in the second game of a doubleheader against the Yankees on July 27, 1978.

In addition to his six runs batted in, he also had a single for the biggest offensive day of his career.

It was the third time in the 20th century a major league player hit two triples in one game.

The first one came in the first inning, the second one in the fifth inning, prompting *Plain Dealer* reporter Dan Coughlin to compose the following poem to start off his story:

Total chaos reigned supreme,
Kuiper had a hitter's dream.
Driving six runs across the plate,
helping seal the Yankees' fate.

Kuiper, of course, is more famous for the fact that he had just one home run in 3,379 at-bats.

(sharing that award with Toby Harrah). He also was an All-Star in 1984. How dangerous of a hitter was he? In 1984, he drew six walks in a game that went into extra innings.

Perhaps his most amazing statistic was his 15 game-winning RBIs in 1982, which set a club record that still stands. Thornton admitted he did approach an at-bat differently in those clutch situations.

"That's your job," he said. "Your role changes. Growing up, every player learned you had to get that runner home however you could. A lot of it depended on the toughness of the pitcher: How much did I have to give up to get that runner home? It didn't matter if you were a power hitter. In that situation, you had to put the ball in play. That was your only job at that point—to get the run in however you could. The third, fourth, and fifth slots in the lineup were run-producing slots. They were all in there for specific

ANDRE THORNTON CAREER STATISTICS

Year	Team	Lg	G	AB	R	H	2B	3B	HR	RBI	SB	CS	BB	SO	BA
1973	CHC	NL	17	35	3	7	3	0	0	2	0	0	7	9	.200
1974	CHC	NL	107	303	41	79	16	4	10	46	2	1	48	50	.261
1975	CHC	NL	120	372	70	109	21	4	18	60	3	2	88	63	.293
1976	TOT	NL	96	268	28	52	11	2	11	38	4	1	48	46	.194
1976	CHC	NL	27	85	8	17	6	0	2	14	2	0	20	14	.200
	MON	NL	69	183	20	35	5	2	9	24	2	1	28	32	.191
1977	CLE	AL	131	433	77	114	20	5	28	70	3	4	70	82	.263
1978	CLE	AL	145	508	97	133	22	4	33	105	4	7	93	72	.262
1979	CLE	AL	143	515	89	120	31	1	26	93	5	4	90	93	.233
1981	CLE	AL	69	226	22	54	12	0	6	30	3	1	23	37	.239
1982	CLE	AL	161	589	90	161	26	1	32	116	6	7	109	81	.273
1983	CLE	AL	141	508	78	143	27	1	17	77	4	2	87	72	.281
1984	CLE	AL	155	587	91	159	26	0	33	99	6	5	91	79	.271
1985	CLE	AL	124	461	49	109	13	0	22	88	3	2	47	75	.236
1986	CLE	AL	120	401	49	92	14	0	17	66	4	1	65	67	.229
1987	CLE	AL	36	85	8	10	2	0	0	5	1	0	10	25	.118
14 Seasons			1565	5291	792	1342	244	22	253	895	48	37	876	851	.254

reasons. Runs win games. I don't care if you hit .300. In those situations, you had to get the runner across the plate. I came up in the Phillies system. I played for Gene Mauch. In those days when you got a guy on base, you'd bunt him over, move him to third, and then score him with a sacrifice fly. That was the way you were expected to play. If you struck out three or four times with runners in scoring position you might not play the next day."

Thornton thinks things have changed considerably since he played. Home runs have become more of a tool today. Pitchers don't seem quite as focused on not letting the big guns hurt them. There's less hostility between teams and, of course, the rules have changed to make sure that's the case. Now a pitcher who gives up one home run and then throws at the next batter will be thrown out of the game. In Thornton's day, that was business as usual.

In some ways, it's amusing to hear him talk of those days in those terms. After all, this is a man who was as well known for his faith as for his intensity and skills. This is a man who was one of the first to speak about his religion and push for pregame chapel services. This is the man who spoke at the memorial service when pitchers Steve Olin and Tim Crews were killed in a tragic boating accident during spring training in 1993.

But his trip down memory lane doesn't last long. When asked to look back on his career, he smiles and says, "It was nice, but I'll never pass down that road again." Even when asked about being inducted into the Indians Hall of Fame, he tries to deflect most of the credit to those who selected him.

"I felt very humbled," he said. "Very appreciative of the fact they considered me worthy of that honor."

MORE CLUTCH PERFORMERS
Sandy Alomar

The Indians fell two outs short of winning the 1997 World Series, but it wasn't for lack of trying by Sandy Alomar Jr. The Indians' popular catcher—the undisputed leader of the team—set career highs with a .324 batting average, 21 home runs, and 83 RBIs, the franchise record for a catcher. He also had a 30-game hitting

Sandy Alomar Jr. celebrates driving in the winning run in the ninth inning of Game 4 of the American League Championship Series at Jacobs Field in Cleveland on October 12, 1997.

streak, second longest in team history. He was named an All-Star and the team's Man of the Year. And who can forget the two-run home run he hit in the seventh inning that lifted the American League to a 3–1 victory in the 68th All-Star Game, which just happened to be held at Jacobs Field? Alomar was voted MVP of that game in a vote by the media—the only Indian MVP and the only player ever so honored in his home ballpark. He was the first Indian to hit a home run in the All-Star Game since Rocky Colavito did it in 1959.

Travis Hafner

Too bad Travis Hafner missed the final 29 games of the 2006 season with a hairline fracture in the fourth metacarpal of his right hand, or there is no telling how many records he might have broken.

As it was, Hafner hit six grand slams in 2006, tying the major league record set by Don Mattingly with the New York Yankees in 1987. For the season, Hafner hit .571 (8 of 14) with six home runs and 30 RBIs with the bases loaded. Overall, Hafner hit .308 (140-for-454) with 31 doubles, 1 triple, 42 home runs, and 117 RBIs in 129 games. His 42 home runs tied for the eighth highest total in club history with Hal Trosky in 1936 and Rocky Colavito in 1959. Hafner also set single-season club records for homers (39) and RBIs (110) as a designated hitter, breaking Andre Thornton's 1982 records. When he got hurt, Hafner was leading the AL in slugging percentage (.659) and on-base percentage (.439) and was ranked second in the AL in home runs and extra base hits (74) and third in RBIs. He is just the second Indian ever with 40 home runs, 100 walks, 100 runs, and 100 RBIs in the same season, joining Jim Thome, who accomplished that feat in 1997, 2001, and 2002. Hafner finished eighth in the AL MVP voting for 2006.

Eddie Murray

The numbers say it all for this Hall of Famer. In a 21-year career, only three of which were spent in Cleveland, Murray became the all-time career RBI leader among switch-hitters with 1,917. He finished his career with 3,026 games, 3,255 hits, 504 home runs, a .287 batting average, and a .476 slugging percentage. He is one of only three players to have totaled 3,000 hits and 500 home runs, along with Hank Aaron and Willie Mays. He was named to eight All-Star teams, won three Gold Glove Awards at first base, and had six consecutive top-10 finishes in voting for the MVP award. The AL Rookie of the Year in 1977 with Baltimore, he batted .300 or more seven times and drove in 100 or more runs six times.

Pat Tabler

Tabler did a little bit of everything in his six seasons with the Indians. A native of Hamilton, Ohio, he played first, second, and third base, as well at the outfield, and was used as a designated hitter. He was never more dangerous than when he came to the plate with the bases loaded. In five-plus seasons with Cleveland, 1983–88, he went 29 for 55 (.527) with the bases loaded. He was an AL All-Star in 1987, when he batted .307. He also batted .326 in 1986.

NUMBERS DON'T LIE [OR DO THEY?]

HOMERS ARE A HIT

It was right there in black and white, but Jim Thome still had trouble believing it.

In one of his most memorable performances with the Indians, Thome had four home runs and 10 RBIs in the 1999 AL Division Series against Boston. That gave him 16 home runs in postseason play, moving him ahead of Babe Ruth into third place in major league history, behind Reggie Jackson and Mickey Mantle, with 18 apiece.

"Look, I am a guy from Peoria, Illinois," an incredulous Thome told reporters after he hit his 14th postseason home run, a grand slam off John Wasdin in the fourth inning of Game 2, becoming the first player to hit two grand slams in his postseason career. "Never, ever, growing up as a kid, did I think my name would someday be mentioned in the same sentence with guys like Babe Ruth, Mickey Mantle, or Reggie Jackson."

Thome later moved within one of Jackson and Mantle with another home run in the 2001 AL Division Series against Seattle. Clearly, he is one of the best home-run hitters in Major League Baseball history, not just Indians history.

His home runs were one of the main reasons Thome was such a popular player in Cleveland. He is the team's all-time leading home-run hitter with 334, followed by Albert Belle with 242, and Manny Ramirez with 236. Though all three moved on to different

Jim Thorne watches the trajectory of his two-run home run off New York Yankees pitcher Roger Clemens on July 2, 2002, at Yankee Stadium. Thome had homered in six straight games, setting a Cleveland record.

teams and got mixed reactions upon their returns to Cleveland, they were all treated like kings while they were here.

Indians fans have long had a love affair with their sluggers, dating back to 1902 and 1903, when Bill Bradley and Charles Hickman hit 11 and 12 homers, respectively, enough to lead the team each of those seasons. From Earl Averill to Hal Trosky to Ken Keltner to Larry Doby to Al Rosen, the long ball has been the shortest route to the hearts of Indians faithful. Seven times Indians players have led or been tied for the AL lead in home runs. Two of the most cherished memories in team history occurred on June 10, 1959, when Rocky Colavito hit four home runs in one game in Baltimore, and on July 31, 1963, when Woodie Held, Pedro Ramos, Tito Francona, and Larry Brown hit four straight home runs in the sixth inning of a game against the Los Angeles Angels. Forty-nine times an Indians player has hit 30 or more home runs in a season, and 29 times a player has hit three home runs in a game.

As respected as the great pitcher Bob Feller is, slugger Colavito may be even more beloved. After all, popular author and former *Akron Beacon Journal* columnist Terry Pluto didn't write a book on Feller. He did write *The Curse of Rocky Colavito: A Loving Look at a Thirty-Year Slump*. And when things turned around in the mid-1990s, he wrote another book titled *Burying the Curse*.

Pluto, who has since moved to *The Plain Dealer*, doesn't mince words. In the introduction to the first book, he writes, "'Don't knock the Rock' probably were not the first words I said, but they are the first I remember. The Indians didn't knock the Rock, they just traded him. The date was April 17, 1960. It was the day Cleveland baseball died, or at least went into a deep, dark, seemingly endless coma."

Pluto is not alone. Indians fans of a certain age—say over 50— were devastated at the loss of Colavito, who tied Harmon Killebrew to lead the American League with 42 home runs in 1959, just his fifth year in the league. When the Indians finally broke out of that 30-year slump, they did so with a bang—provided by the bats of Thome and Belle and Ramirez.

The three players could not have been more different.

Much like Colavito, Thome and Cleveland were a perfect fit. The native of Peoria, Illinois, was the kind of hardworking regular guy made to play in a blue-collar, lunch-bucket-carrying town like Cleveland.

DID YOU KNOW...

That the Indians' single-season home-run record is 52, hit by by Jim Thome in 2002?

Thome was born on August 27, 1970, three minutes after his twin sister Jennifer. He was a 1988 graduate of Limestone (Illinois) High School, where he was all-state in baseball and basketball. He played both sports at Illinois Central and was an honorable mention junior college All-American in baseball.

He was drafted by the Indians in the 13th round of the 1989 amateur draft and made his major league debut on September 4,

1991, going 2-for-4 with an RBI in his debut. It was 1994 when he played his first full season in the majors. He was strictly a third baseman at that point, but the Indians used him at third base and as a designated hitter in 1995 and 1996. In 1996, he hit .311 with 38 home runs and 116 RBIs. That was good enough to earn him a Silver Slugger Award as the best-hitting third baseman in the American League. He also finished 15th in the voting for the AL MVP.

INDIANS TOP TEN HOME-RUN HITTERS

Jim Thome 334
Albert Belle 242
Manny Ramirez 236
Earl Averill 226
Hal Trosky 216
Larry Doby 215
Andre Thornton 214
Al Rosen 192
Rocky Colavito 190
Ken Keltner 163

The next season the Indians moved him to first base. He responded with a .286 batting average, 40 home runs, and a league-leading 120 walks. He earned the first of three straight AL All-Star berths and finished sixth in the MVP voting.

From then on, the 6'4", 245-pound Thome became one of the most feared hitters in the AL on one of the league's best teams. He was always among the league leaders in on-base percentage. Twice more he led the league in walks (with 127 in 1999 and 122 in 2002) and was second in home runs with 49 in 2001 and 52 in 2002. He also led the league with a .677 slugging percentage in 2002.

But in addition to all those towering home runs, all those timely walks, it must be noted that Thome remained a down-to-earth, likeable guy—always ready with an autograph or an interview. Some think his willingness to sign all those autographs stems from being snubbed by Dave Kingman when Thome was a young Cubs fan in search of a signature. He also supported numerous charitable projects and won the 2002 Roberto Clemente Award from MLB for his community service.

That proved to be his last season in Cleveland. Although Cleveland fans don't want to hear it, it was a gut-wrenching decision for Thome to leave and sign with the Philadelphia

Phillies. But the Phillies were offering Thome a six-year, $85 million contract, twice as much money as the Indians.

In 2003, he tied Alex Rodriguez for the major league lead in home runs with 47. It was the first time a Philadelphia player led the National League in home runs since Mike Schmidt hit 37 in 1986. Thome finished fourth in the NL MVP voting, the highest finish for a Phillie since Lenny Dykstra finished second to Pittsburgh's Barry Bonds in 1993.

His numbers dipped a tad in 2004, when he hit 42 home runs with 105 RBIs, but he still earned his first NL All-Star berth. In 2005, he was plagued by back and elbow problems, which limited him to a career-low 59 games. Still, in a survey of players by the Tribune Company, Thome was named the best teammate in Major League Baseball. After being traded to the White Sox, he was named the 2006 Comeback Player of the Year after batting .288 with 42 home runs, 109 RBIs, 108 runs scored, and 107 walks in his first season with Chicago.

Belle and Ramirez were polar opposites. Anything and everything could upset Belle; nothing seemed to bother Ramirez.

Belle and his twin brother, Terry, were born in Shreveport, Louisiana, on August 25, 1966. Belle, who went by the name of Joey until early in his major league career, was a two-time all-state baseball player at Huntington High School, where he also played football and was a member of the National Honor Society. He was first-team All-Southeastern Conference in 1986 and 1987 at Louisiana State University, where he had a combined .332 batting average and .670 slugging average with 49 home runs and 172 RBIs. He was drafted by the Indians in the second round of the 1987 draft and two years later, he was in the major leagues. By 1993, he made the first of five straight All-Star appearances. He was feared as much for his hitting as for his temper.

Ramirez was born to Aristides and Onelcida Ramirez on May 30, 1972, in Santo Domingo, Dominican Republic. He played baseball almost every day. When he was 13, he and his three sisters joined their parents in Washington Heights, New York, on the Upper West Side of Manhattan, not far from Yankee Stadium.

He enrolled in George Washington High School and led his team to three straight Manhattan Division championships and to the Division finals in 1991, when he was named High School Player of the Year in the New York City Public Schools. In June 1991, the Indians selected Ramirez in the first round (13th overall) of the MLB amateur draft. He made his major league debut with an inauspicious 0-for-4 appearance against Minnesota on September 2, 1993. The next night he hit two home runs and a ground rule double against the Yankees in New York—and he never stopped hitting after that. He led the team in home runs in 1998 (45), 1999 (44), and 2000 (38) and is the Indians all-time leader in slugging percentage at .592. On December 12, 2000, Ramirez signed a $160 million, eight-year contract to play with the Boston Red Sox, helping the team win the 2004 World Series and being named the Series MVP. Somewhere along the way, he stopped talking to reporters. His occasionally odd behavior is dismissed with the saying, "Manny being Manny."

> # TRIVIA
>
> Who set the major league record for grand slams in a season that Travis Hafner tied in 2006?
>
> Find the answers on pages 159–160.

Into the void left by the departures of Belle, Ramirez, and Thome stepped Travis Hafner. In demeanor and approach, he reminds many of Thome, a small-town boy who brings a blue-collar work ethic to the game. Hafner was born June 3, 1977, in Jamestown, North Dakota, and grew up in Sykeston, where there were eight kids in his graduating class—four boys and four girls. "Everybody had a date for the prom," he once told reporters.

Wrote *Plain Dealer* columnist Bill Livingston, shortly after Hafner signed a $57 million contract extension that could keep him with the Indians through 2013, "He is as small town as a bake sale to raise money so the band can go to the big out-of-town game."

At Sykeston High School, Hafner earned all-region honors in basketball and finished third in the state in the discus and triple jump as a senior before attending Cowley County Community

College in Arkansas City, Kansas, where he was the MVP of the JUCO World Series as Cowley won the title in 1997. He was selected by the Texas Rangers in the 31st round of the June draft in 1996 and traded to the Indians with pitcher Aaron Myette for pitcher Ryan Drese and catcher Einar Diaz on December 6, 2002. Somewhere along the line he picked up the nickname "Pronk," for "part project, part donkey." But the project part seems to be finished, since he has hit so many home runs into the upper deck in right field in Jacobs Field that they've named it "Pronkville" in his honor.

He had a career year in 2006, when he set single-season designated hitter club records for home runs (39) and RBIs (110). (He hit a total of 42 home runs in 2006, three of which came with him playing first base.) He finished eighth in the AL MVP voting and just missed making the All-Star team. He also tied a major league record with six grand slams in one season.

Like Thome, Averill, and Colavito before him, Hafner is a perfect fit here.

"He does fit Cleveland," manager Eric Wedge told Livingston. "He shows up every day, and you know what you're going to get from him. A lot of people in this city have those same qualities."

A GREAT BARGAIN
Bob Feller is Mr. Indian

No player is more respected or has done more for the franchise than the great pitcher who was 16 years old in 1935 when he signed with the team for $1 and an autographed baseball. In 2007, 71 years after his first season with the team and 51 after his last season with the team, Feller still leads the Indians in innings pitched (3,827), wins (266), strikeouts (2,581), complete games (279), games started (484), and All-Star appearances (8, including starts in 1941 and 1946). He won 20 or more games six times, including a career-high 27 in 1940. He was the Major League Player of the Year in 1940 and was voted the Indians Man of the Year in 1951, when he also was named the AL Pitcher of the Year.

Bob Feller, the 19-year-old schoolboy hurler from Van Meter, Iowa, shows off his high-kick pitching motion at spring training in New Orleans on February 28, 1938.

Although many great players have starred with the team through the years, in 2006 fans voted Feller the Indians Hometown Hero, the player who most represents the franchise. In 1969 fans voted him the greatest living right-handed pitcher as part of baseball's centennial celebration.

Hardly a day goes by that Feller, who will turn 90 in 2008, isn't doing something for the franchise, whether it's making a personal appearance or signing an autograph.

MVP VOTES

Since the MVP awards were established in 1931, six players have received 400 or more votes while wearing Indian uniforms:

- 896—Lou Boudreau, 1940–49 (won the award in 1948)
- 838—Bob Feller, 1939–51
- 835—Albert Belle, 1992–96
- 559—Bob Lemon, 1948–56
- 480—Manny Ramirez, 1995–2000
- 414—Al Rosen, 1950–54 (won the award in 1953)

"You never want to leave your house or your hotel room without a couple pens in your pocket," the Hall of Famer said, laughing. "It goes with the territory. You have to accept that. Being in the public eye, the pluses far exceed the minuses."

Feller has been in the public eye since famed Indians scout Cy Slapnicka stumbled upon Feller while looking for another pitcher.

According to *The Cleveland Indians* by Franklin Lewis, Slapnicka hurried back to Cleveland, where he told the team's board of directors, "Gentlemen, I've found the greatest young pitcher I ever saw. I suppose this sounds like the same old stuff to you, but I want you to believe me. This boy that I found out in Iowa will be the greatest pitcher the world has ever known.

"I found this boy, name of Bob Feller, in a small town not far from Des Moines—Van Meter, they call it. I know that country out there pretty well. My home section, you see. Well, my friends told me about this boy, so I went to see him pitch. I only saw him pitch once before I signed him. Went back to the Feller farm that same night and the boy's father and I made a deal."

The signing of Feller on July 25, 1935, did not come off without a hitch. At the time, baseball rules prohibited major league teams from signing sandlot players. When a minor league team in Iowa tried to sign Feller in 1935, his contract with the Indians came to light. The Iowa team complained to Judge

Kenesaw Mountain Landis, the baseball commissioner. Landis could have voided Feller's contract and declared him a free agent. But Feller told Landis he wanted to stay with the Indians, so Landis fined the team $7,500, which was awarded to Iowa.

Feller, born November 13, 1918, was so young his father had to co-sign the contract. In some ways, that was only fitting since it was his father who bought the nine-year-old Feller his first flannel uniform from a mail-order catalog, who persuaded him to become a pitcher instead of a shortstop when he was 15, and who built him his own ballpark on their farm 20 miles west of Des Moines, a park that served as the model for the one in the movie *Field of Dreams*. The farm had no electricity or indoor plumbing, but it was the perfect place for Feller and his sister, Marguerite, to grow up. His dad was a farmer. His mother was a teacher and a registered nurse, but she quit working so she could be there when her children got home from school.

After signing with the Indians, Feller, who threw five no-hitters in high school, pitched in the state high school tournament in 1936, then went to the Indians and struck out eight in three innings of exhibition game against the St. Louis Cardinals. In his first start, on August 23, 1936, he threw a six-hitter and struck out 15 St. Louis Browns in a 4–1 victory, just missing the American League record of 16 strikeouts. In his fifth start, he threw a two-hitter and struck out 17 Philadelphia Athletics in a 5–2 victory to tie Dizzy Dean's single-game record. He finished his first season 5–3.

In all the books and stories written about Feller, there is no mention that he was ever homesick or unsure of himself despite leaving home at the age of 17. Slapnicka and his wife, along with trainer Lefty Weisman and his family, took the young Feller under their wings, and they seemed to be enough for him.

> **TRIVIA**
>
> When did Bob Feller make his professional debut?
> Find the answers on pages 159–160.

"My mother hated that I never got homesick," Feller admitted. "She said, 'All those years I brought that kid up and he didn't even miss me.' But when I was a kid about nine, I read something Thomas Edison said: Find out what you want to do with your life and do it and never work again. That's what I did."

After his first season, the 6'0", 185-pound Feller (who earned the nickname "Rapid Robert" for his fastball delivery) went back home to Van Meter. Despite starting his senior year several weeks late, he was voted president of his class of 17. Then he left for spring training in February, where he was the only player with a tutor making him do his homework. All told, he had a five-month senior year. Unfortunately, early in the 1937 season he slipped while throwing a pitch in the rain and hurt his arm and was out for two months. That did allow him to return to Van Meter for his high school graduation, which was covered by NBC Radio. Think of the worldwide coverage such an event would attract these days.

He returned to the Indians, and later that season in a game against the New York Yankees, with the score tied 1–1 in the ninth inning, he threw a change up that Joe DiMaggio knocked out of the park for a grand slam in a 5–1 victory. After the game, some of the Yankees said Feller didn't belong in the majors and should be in the minors, which fueled his rivalry with DiMaggio and the Indians' rivalry with the Yankees.

It was a good thing the Indians didn't listen to the Yankees. Feller went 9–7 in 1937. On October 1, 1938, the last day of the season, Feller struck out 18 Detroit Tigers to set the major league record for that time. He finished that season 17–11, went 24–9 in 1939, 27–11 in 1940, including the only Opening Day no-hitter in the history of Major League Baseball, and 25–13 in 1941.

Then the most amazing thing happened. Two days after the Japanese bombed Pearl Harbor, Feller, the preeminent pitcher of his time, enlisted in the navy. As the sole support of his family back in Iowa, he would not have had to go. But he felt it was his patriotic duty to do so. He wanted no part of a stateside desk job, either. He served 44 months, most of them aboard the USS *Alabama*, earning eight battle stars as a chief gunnery officer.

Feller missed nearly four full seasons, pitching in just a handful of games at the end of the 1945 season. In his first game back, on August 24, 1945, a crowd of 46,477 watched Feller strike

THE NEXT BIG THING

It's not just that C.C. Sabathia is 6'7" and weighs nearly 300 pounds.

It's that his powerful left arm has made him the ace of the Indians pitching staff and one of the best pitchers in Major League Baseball as well as the 2007 Cy Young Award winner.

"C.C. wants to be the man...," Indians manager Eric Wedge has said, "and I love him for it."

Sabathia started off with a bang. As a rookie in 2001, he went 17–5 with a 4.39 ERA and 171 strikeouts in 180½ innings to help the team win its sixth Central Division title in seven years. He finished second to Seattle's Ichiro Suzuki in voting for the AL Rookie of the Year.

His record dipped to 13–11 in 2002, but he was 13–9 in 2003 and 11–10 in 2004, making the All-Star team both seasons. He had a 15–10 season in 2005 and a 12–11 season in 2006, when he led Major League Baseball with six complete games and tied for first in the AL with two shutouts. He also ranked third in the AL with a 3.22 ERA.

In another All-Star season in 2007, he reached double-digit victories (a career-high 19) for the seventh straight season, the only left-handed Indian to do so and just the second Cleveland pitcher to do so, joining Hall of Famer Addie Joss, who accomplished that feat in his first eight seasons. He led all major leaguers under the age of 28 in wins and strikeouts and was second in innings pitched.

"I want to be a Roger Clemens–type pitcher," he once said. "When Roger Clemens or Curt Schilling or Randy Johnson take the mound, you pretty much know they're going to win that game. And when I take the mound I want my teammates to say, 'OK, we're going to win this game.'"

When he gets the chance he can hit, too. Since interleague play began in 1997, Sabathia leads all AL pitchers with a .297 batting average, 11 hits, 6 RBIs, and a .405 slugging percentage. He hit a home run against Cincinnati on May 21, 2005, and even was called on to pinch hit (he singled) in a 16-inning game in Pittsburgh in 2003.

Sabathia has been bothered by some injuries, but after New York's Tom Glavine won his 300th game during the 2007 season, the 27-year-old Sabathia said he'd love to pitch long enough to have a shot to join Glavine in that elite club.

"I'm going to try to play," he said, "until my arm falls off."

out 12 Tigers in a 4–2 victory over rival Hal Newhouser. He finished that season 5–3, setting the stage for his historic performance in 1946, when he went 26–15 with a then-record 348 strikeouts and a 2.18 earned-run average and led the American League in wins, shutouts (10), strikeouts, games pitched (48), and innings (371.1).

Some estimate that Feller would have had 100 or more victories had he not enlisted, but Feller could not care less.

"I made a lot of mistakes in my life," he said. "Joining the navy two days after Pearl Harbor was not one of them."

Thanks to the talents of Feller and his teammates, the Indians became one of the dominant teams in baseball, winning the World Series in 1948 and returning in 1954, only to be swept by the New York Giants. Feller, though, never was able to win a World Series game. In 1948, a controversial call by umpire Bill Stewart allowed pinch runner Phil Masi to score the game's only run in the eighth inning of Game 1 against the Boston Braves. Feller, who pitched a two-hitter, and Lou Boudreau thought they had picked off Masi at second base, and photos indicated they had. But Stewart called Masi safe. In later years, Masi admitted he was out, and Stewart admitted he made a mistake. Feller also lost Game 5, 11–5. Though he had a 13–3 record in the regular season, manager Al Lopez didn't call on him to pitch in the 1954 World Series. Feller said he was never told why, and he never asked.

Feller, who was instrumental in the creation of the baseball players association and the pension plan, retired after the 1956 season, and his career has been unmatched. He finished with a 266–162 record, 3.25 ERA, and .621 winning percentage. He had three no-hitters and 12 one-hitters. He led the league in wins six times and in strikeouts seven times. He threw a fastball 104 miles per hour, faster than a speeding motorcycle, during a promotional stunt in Chicago's Lincoln Park in 1940, and hit 107.9 at the Aberdeen Ordnance Plant in Washington, D.C., the fastest pitch ever measured with a speed measuring device. He was inducted into the Hall of Fame in 1962 on the first ballot, and he was the first player to have his number (19) retired by the Indians in 1957. The only reason he never won a Cy Young Award was that it wasn't established until the year he retired. In addition to retiring his No. 19, the Indians honored Feller by placing a 10-foot-tall bronze statue of him at the East Ninth Street entrance to Jacobs Field.

"It's nice to be immortalized when you're still alive," Feller said.

MASS APPEAL

455.

It was an honor, a tribute, a way of life.

For five and a half seasons, in spite of heat and humidity or wind and snow, every seat at Jacobs Field was filled. From June 12, 1995, until April 4, 2001, for a total of 455 games, the Indians sold out their stadium, setting a major league record.

In reality, the feat was more about the fans than the team. Shivering through one spring or fall in Ohio is all it takes to understand why.

Yes, these were the Indians of Albert Belle and Jim Thome, Manny Ramirez and Omar Vizquel, Charlie Nagy, Jaret Wright, and Bartolo Colon. During the stretch, their teams never won fewer than 86 games in a season, finished in first place five times in six years, and advanced to the World Series twice. Mike Hargrove managed five of those teams, while Charlie Manuel was in charge of one.

But for Cleveland's long-suffering sports fans, it was a chance to show their devotion, to give voice to the throaty cheers that never seemed to be quite enough to help the struggling Browns or the Cavaliers. The city had not won a major championship since the Browns' NFL title in 1964, but no one could blame the fans for not doing everything they could to bring one home. It was impossible to go anywhere in northeast Ohio without running into somebody wearing an Indians jersey or cap. Most businesses promoted Indians days at work, especially on Fridays, when fans were encouraged to wear red in support of the team.

When the Indians drew 41,845 for a game against Baltimore on June 12, 1995, a little more than a year after their beautiful new ballpark opened, no one realized that would be the start of an unprecedented run of sellouts. As it happened, a number of events worked in the team's favor. There was the lure of the powerful team playing in its new home, but the Browns left after the 1995 season and the Cavaliers went into a prolonged slump. All the attention was focused on the Indians, and the team and its fans responded in a big way.

Although the team didn't see the start of the streak coming, the same could not be said for the end. Officials were well aware that after the team failed to make the playoffs after the 2000 season that there would be a drop-off in attendance in 2001. The last sellout in the streak came on Opening Day on April 2, 2001, when 42,606 turned out. But two days later, "just" 32,763 turned out to watch Chuck Finley beat the Chicago White Sox, 8–4.

"I tried not to take it personally," Finley told reporters after the game.

Indians owner Larry Dolan saluted the fans in a message on the scoreboard, and the number 455 was retired to a place of honor, joining those of Bob Feller, Mel Harder, Earl Averill, Lou Boudreau, Larry Doby, and Bob Lemon.

When Nagy was inducted into the Indians Hall of Fame late in the 2007 season, he paid tribute to the fans and the atmosphere they created at the ballpark during their great run.

"It was a joy to be here and come to the park every day to sellout crowds," he said.

IT'S NOT OVER 'TIL IT'S OVER

THE INDIANS' GREATEST COMEBACK

Those who were there still don't believe it, and those who weren't there claimed they were.

It was the topic of conversation for days after the Indians rallied from a 12-run deficit to beat the Seattle Mariners, 15–14, in 11 innings on August 5, 2001. It tied the greatest comeback in major league history. The last team to rally from a 12–0 deficit was the Philadelphia A's against the Indians on June 15, 1925.

"The biggest lesson this game teaches you is to never give up and to keep on swinging," Indians manager Charlie Manuel said after the game. "This may have been the best game I've ever managed. I took all my guys out and didn't have any moves left to make."

In the greatest tribute an event can have these days, ESPN named it an instant classic and replayed it in its entirety—all 4 hours and 11 minutes of it—the next night so Clevelanders could celebrate all over again.

Although the victory improved the Indians' record to 62–48 and got them within a half-game of first-place Minnesota in the AL Central, things had not been going all that well for the team. They'd lost four of the first five games of the homestand and were outscored, 43–18, in doing so.

But at least for one night, the magic was back in Jacobs Field.

"Back in 1994, 1995, and 1996, there was a roar in this park," Manuel told reporters after the game. "You couldn't hear voices, just a roar. Like when you walk on a beach by the ocean. We still get that roar every once in a while now. Tonight we got the roar."

Said reliever Bob Wickman after the game ended at 12:19 AM, "It felt like winning the seventh game of the World Series."

It's not necessary to relive how the Indians fell behind 12–0 after three innings or 14–2 after five. Suffice it to say, starter Dave Burba was not on top of his game.

As *Plain Dealer* columnist Bill Livingston wrote, "Dave Burba, on Indians mascot Slider's 11th birthday, impersonated the piñata at a festive occasion. With fuchsia-colored balloons bobbing in the stands, Burba seemed to suck all the air out of the Indians' season, driven from the mound after surrendering seven runs in just two innings plus three batters of work."

Poor Mike Bacsik, making his major league debut, replaced Burba with no outs and the bases loaded in the third. The Mariners, who came into the game with an 80–30 record, were leading, 4–0. Then Bacsik gave up eight runs (three charged to Burba) and four hits. He pitched in two more games for the Indians that season, wound up with a 9.00 ERA, and was traded to the New York Mets after the season. He eventually gained fame in 2007 for giving up Barry Bonds' record-breaking 756th homer run.

TRIVIA

Who was the winning pitcher for the Indians in their historic comeback?

Find the answers on pages 159–160.

Jim Thome hit a two-run homer off Seattle starter Aaron Sele in the fourth that made it 12–2. After the Mariners scored twice in the top of the fifth, the Indians chased Sele and added three runs in the seventh, led by Russell Branyan's 15th homer, to make it 14–5. Manuel, sensing the inevitable, removed regulars Robbie Alomar, Ellis Burks, and Juan Gonzalez.

But a funny thing happened on the way to the slaughter.

Thome hit his 36th homer to start the eighth. Marty Cordova hit a two-run homer and Omar Vizquel doubled home another

BY THE NUMBERS

393 — Pitches thrown by both teams
232 — Strikes thrown by both teams
111 — Batters faced by both teams, including 54 by the Indians
40 — Hits in the game, including a season-high 23 by Cleveland
28 — Runs batted in and earned runs
27 — Flyball outs
22 — Ground ball outs
18 — Runners left on base
14 — Strikeouts
12 — Pitchers used, including five by Cleveland
7 — Walks

run to make it 14–9. Kenny Lofton was thrown out at home trying to score on a pitch that got away from catcher Tom Lampkin. It seemed like it was just that kind of night.

Only it wasn't.

Eddie Taubensee singled to open the ninth before Norm Charlton, who had relieved John Halama in the eighth, retired the next two batters. Cordova doubled Taubensee to third for his fourth hit of the game. Jeff Nelson relieved, but walked Wil Cordero and gave up a two-run single to Einar Diaz to make it 14–11. Closer Kazuhiro Sasaki relieved to face Lofton, who singled to left to load the bases.

Vizquel worked the count full, and the Indians were down to their last strike. It was all he needed. He hit a three-run triple past Ed Sprague, a diving Seattle first baseman, and into the right-field corner to score Cordero, Diaz, and Lofton.

"No doubt it was my biggest hit of the year," Vizquel said.

The place went bananas—but the Indians weren't finished.

In an odd quirk, *Plain Dealer* columnist Roger Brown reported that ESPN viewers who had turned off the game earlier actually started tuning back in. The night started with a 1.5 rating, dropped to 1.16, and then rebounded to 2.58.

STICK AROUND

On August 23, 2006, the Indians beat the host team, the Kansas City Royals, 15–13, in 10 innings. According to the Elias Sports Bureau, the Indians were only the second team in major league history to win a game after giving up 10 runs in the first inning. (Philadelphia beat Pittsburgh, 15–11, on June 8, 1989.) It was the Indians' biggest comeback since their franchise-record 12-run rally to beat Seattle on August 5, 2001.

It was also the first time in major league history that opposing teams registered double-digit first innings against each other in the same season. On August 13, the Indians scored a season-high 11 runs in the first inning off Kansas City's Luke Hudson.

Viewers who came back to the game were rewarded with the memorable eleventh inning.

Lofton singled to center and went to second on Vizquel's single off Jose Paniagua. Then Jolbert Cabrera, who had replaced Alomar in the sixth, hit Paniagua's first pitch for a broken-bat single to score Lofton with the winning run with one out.

Pandemonium ensued. Lofton, who was 4-for-6 and scored three runs, leaped onto home plate and then jumped into the arms of on-deck hitter Taubensee.

"Kenny was pumped because he had a great night," Taubensee told reporters. "When he scored, he jumped up in the air, and I caught him. I caught him, and I wasn't going to let him go. He was the king of the night, and I was going to let him get all the credit he deserved."

Of his game-winning RBI, Cabrera told reporters, "I got lucky. I put the bat on the ball, and it broke the bat.... I think this can be the turning point of the season."

Sadly, it was not. The magic lasted less than 24 hours. The very next day the Indians lost to the Mariners, 8–6. They fell behind by four runs in the seventh inning.

There was no comeback on that night.

ON THE OTHER HAND

Ironically, until the Indians rallied from a 12-run deficit to beat the Seattle Mariners, 15–14, in 11 innings on August 5, 2001, they had been the victims of the last team to rally from 12 runs down. That occurred against the Athletics in Philadelphia on June 15, 1925.

Not only does that game offer another perspective emotionally for Indians fans, but it allows a look into how things have changed in the world of sportswriting.

The preceding story on the Indians' victory over the Mariners includes excerpts from one of the finest sportswriters at *The Plain Dealer* today. The game story was written by the incomparable Paul Hoynes, one of the best in the business, so good that he was elected president of the Baseball Writers' Association of America. With him at Jacobs Field that night were Bill Livingston, the newspaper's venerable columnist who never fails to deliver in the clutch, and Tim Warsinskey, a rising star who was assigned to provide a sidebar. While the personnel might change from game to game, the trio of lead writer, columnist, and sidebar writer was the standard operating procedure for *The Plain Dealer* at most home games.

On the road, however, Hoynes usually was by himself, as was the equally legendary Stuart M. Bell that day in Philadelphia. For the differences in their styles, and in the times, one need read no more than the first few paragraphs.

Wrote Hoynes in *The Plain Dealer* on August 6, 2001:

Manager Charlie Manuel heard the roar last night at Jacobs Field.

It came from the fans as the Indians rallied from a 12–0 deficit to beat Seattle, 15–14, in 11 innings. It ties the biggest comeback in big-league history.

"Back in 1994, 1995 and 1996, there was a roar in this park," said Manuel. "You couldn't hear voices, just a roar. Like when you walk on a beach by the ocean.

"We still get that roar every once in a while now. Tonight we got the roar."

Jolbert Cabrera, who replaced Robbie Alomar in the sixth when the game was seemingly lost, singled home

Kenny Lofton celebrates after scoring the winning run in the eleventh inning against the Seattle Mariners on August 5, 2001. The Indians tied a major league record in the game and became the first team in 76 years to overcome a 12-run deficit to win, defeating the Mariners 15–14.

Kenny Lofton with the winning run with one out. Lofton started the rally with a single to center and went to second on Omar Vizquel's single off Jose Paniagua (3–3).

The victory pulled them to within a half-game of first-place Minnesota in the American League Central.

Hoynes story featured the common structure of modern sports stories: short, punchy lead, followed by a quote, followed by what editors like to call "the nut graph" that contains all the basic information and an update on the standings.

My how things have changed in 76 years.
Wrote Bell in *The Plain Dealer* on June 16, 1925:

Philadelphia, June 15—Like the deceased gentleman who suddenly woke up to read his own obituary, the Athletics, who had played dead here this afternoon for seven innings, came to life in the eighth and scored thirteen runs, enough to beat the Indians, 17 to 15.

The details, cruel but true, will be found in another column and describe more fully the sad event. This story can only serve to amplify the details, which to Clevelanders will read gruesomely, and to Philadelphians, joyously.

This unexpected orgy of the Athletics broke out late in the matinee, after the writing fraternity had written pages and reams of words about the farcical contest which had taken the Men of Mack out of first place, given Walter Miller, the young collegian, his third straight victory, and placed the Indians one notch nearer third place in the American League race.

Bell's game story, typical of his era, reads much more like what we would call a review or a column today, since he uses some opinionated adjectives (cruel, sad) and inserts himself (as a member of the writing fraternity) into the event. It certainly makes for enjoyable reading, just different. There are no quotes, also typical. On those rare occasions when quotes are used, they are saved for the sidebars. There are some minor style differences as well, including the spelling out of numbers (thirteen runs) and the omission of the hyphen in the final score (17 to 15, numbers obviously used for scores). Also, some first names are missing entirely, while in other instances Bell uses "Mr. Mack" or "Mr. Uhle."

The placement of the stories is interesting as well. Although there's a headline above the front-page masthead on August 6, 2001, that read, "Tribe Pulls Record Comeback for 15–14 Win!", the story is contained in the sports section. Bell's story starts on the bottom of the front page, between two house ads, which typically

BIGGEST DEFICIT OVERCOME TO WIN A GAME: 12 RUNS

August 5, 2001

Seattle	0 4 8	0 2 0	0 0 0	0 0	14
Cleveland	0 0 0	2 0 0	3 4 5	0 1	15

June 15, 1925

Cleveland	0 4 2	2 4 2	1 0 0		15
Philadelphia	0 1 1	0 0 1	1 13 x		17

June 18, 1911

Chicago	7 0 0	3 3 0	2 0 0		15
Detroit	0 1 0	0 4 3	0 5 3		16

are used to plug space. One touts the newspaper's sports section, while the other is for the used car section of the classified ads. Bell's story was one of a dozen or so stories that started on the front page that day, including a murder trial in Chicago and a lightning strike that killed a local man. Curiously, the story starts one column away from a short reference box on the game that directs readers to the sports pages.

Bell's story jumps to page 18, and the inside pages more closely resemble today's sports pages with stories and box scores, although the columns are narrower—eight to a page instead of today's six. One notable difference is the photographs. Today's technology allows for up-to-the-minute action shots—in color— on the inside pages. In 1925, the paper featured still photographs that could be plugged in as necessary. For instance, accompanying Bell's story is a black-and-white stock cutout photo of Charlie Jamieson swinging a bat, with a cutline that points out he had five hits in six at-bats. One problem: the nameplate accompanying the photo spells his name "Charlie" while the game story and the cutline spell it "Charley."

An idea that seems to have stood the test of time was the note-book that ran with the game story. In today's *Plain Dealer*, the notebooks—stories made up of a series of small anecdotes, statistics, or quotes that might not otherwise make the paper—that run with Indians game stories are labeled "Indians Insider." Bell's notebook was neither labeled nor bylined. It included five small items, ranging from an injury to umpire Clarence Owens, who was run over by Indians second baseman Fred Spurgeon, to a women's drill team from Cleveland that attended the game to updates on hitting streaks, double-play totals, and a 30-year-old rookie pitcher for Philadelphia. But in another curious layout, one column away and under Jamieson's picture was a single-paragraph story on Philadelphia manager Connie Mack declaring injured first baseman Joe Hauser retired that would have seemed perfect fodder for the notebook.

At any rate, because it's so different and such an enjoyable read, what follows is the rest of Bell's story verbatim. Also, did you ever think you'd hear Philadelphia referred to as a "burgh of quiet Quakers"? Must have been a long, long time ago.

After Al Simmons, the Mackian wrecker, had lifted the ball over the roof of the left field stands for a home run that scored two runners ahead of him, writers tore up their epitaphs and started new ones to tell how the Macks came from behind and won in a rally, the like of which had never been before seen in this burgh of quiet Quakers.

One would not have given a plugged dime, or even a plugged nickel, for the Athletics' chances to win after the Indians, in their first real batting debauch of the season, had larruped five of Mr. Mack's pitchers for twenty-three hits and fifteen runs. When the eighth opened, the league leaders had made only four runs off Walter Miller, who had pitched courageously and effectively in some spots and not so well in others.

He began to weaken in the sixth, not so much from any stick barrage the Macks had been laying but from the terrific heat. After he had walked two men and allowed a single and triple in the eighth without getting any more than one out, Manager Speaker derricked him

DID YOU KNOW...

That the 1925 Indians team had one of the best starts in team history? They started the season 11–4, a record they matched in 1930, 1935, 1938, 1941, 1948, 1959, 1998, and 2002. Their best start was 14–1 in 1966. They were 12–3 in 1942, 1988, and 1999.

and substituted Bryon Speece, who was back in uniform this afternoon for the first time in three weeks.

Mr. Speece stayed in long enough to give up three hits and then Carl Yowell was substituted. Carl walked a batter and allowed a hit and George Uhle, flower of Mr. Speaker's casting corps, ascended the dais.

Mr. Uhle, despite his nonchalance, his experience and his skill, could not stop the Mackian hitters, who were drunk with their suddenly awakened batting punch. Another man was retired after Uhle came in with French, a runner for Dykes still on first. Uhle held Lamar's hitting ability in high respect, walking him to take a chance on Simmons, a right handed batter.

Mr. Simmons did not waste any time in settling the issue. He crashed, hit the bat against the second pitch and the three runners, French, Lamar and Simmons, circled the paths amid the maddest frenzy of cheering that staid old Philadelphia has ever been witness to.

After seeing today's game, it is easy to understand the big-run games which Chicago and Philadelphia put on here. Big scores here are not entirely a matter of hitting: Lady Luck plays a big part.

The infield and outfield at Shibe Park are treacherous battle grounds, the inner diamond being rough and tricky, and the outer garden hard from continuous baking of the sun.

Several of Cleveland's hits in the early innings skidded past infielders, and Joe Sewell's home run in the third inning came as a result of the ball going over Simmons' head in one bound for a roll to the flag pole.

Lady Luck, so good to the Indians in the first seven innings, turned against them in the eighth, and twice when the tribe had chances to retire the side the fickle dame waved her wand and easy infield chances shot to the outfield for base hits.

Simmons' first hit in the eighth was a grounder on which the ball bounded over Knode's head. Sewell was all set to field Pinch Hitter Hael's grounder for a double play but the ball hit something and also bounced over Joe's head to center field. The only satisfaction the Indians got out of the holocaust was the emergence from their long batting lethargy. Everybody on the team except those three who got into the game after the eighth, made one or more hits. Charley Jamieson came so far out of his slump that he made five consecutive hits, while Joe Sewell made four in a row. Jamieson stole two bases, Lutske one and Myatt one. When the Tribe got tired hitting the ball on the nose they started laying it down for safe bunts and put over one double steal for a tally. Cliff Lee and Jamieson each drove in three runs, Lee getting a double, triple and sacrifice fly, but where they worked all afternoon for their laurels, Al Simmons, still persimmons to the Indians, drove in a trio of tallies with one deathly blow.

TWO MORE GAMES FOR THE AGES

The following two games did not involve record performances. The Indians came back farther to win and gave up more runs in losing. They scored more runs in an inning, and they gave up more runs in an inning.

They are about two spectacular comebacks, but what makes them truly spectacular is the writing. They are included here in their entirety for the pure enjoyment reading them will bring. To recount the details in different words would not do the games, or the writers, justice. Prolific author (and former *Plain Dealer* writer and columnist) Russell Schneider, who actually signed a minor league contract with the Indians as a young catcher, included parts of them in *The Cleveland Indians Encyclopedia,* and it's easy to see why. The first, without a byline, runs on page 437 under a headline proclaiming it "Major League Baseball's most bizarre game in 1901." The second, by the delightful Bell, is on page 438 and concerns "the wildest opener in major league history in 1925."

As with Bell's story on the Indians squandering a 12-run lead in 1924, there are the notable style differences and some curious turns of phrase. In the previous story, for instance, Bell refers to Al Simmons as "persimmons" to the Indians, referring to the sour taste of the fruit before it ripens. In the following story on the big comeback in 1901, the unnamed writer refers to a "Sheridan in the form of a batting rally arrived," apparently a reference to Union general Philip Henry Sheridan, who helped defeat Robert E. Lee in the Civil War.

TRIVIA

The 1901 team started 4–16. What's the only Indians team with a worse record after the first 20 games of the season?

Find the answers on pages 159–160.

Then again, readers in those days probably wouldn't understand our modern references to things like *American Idol.* It makes no difference. The stories, and the writers, still stand the tests of time.

On May 23, 1901, under the headline "Never Too Late to Win, Cleveland Made the Most Wonderful Finish on Record, Nine Runs After All Seemed Over," *The Plain Dealer* told of the Indians' rally for a 14–13 victory over Washington.

There was a baseball game at League Park yesterday afternoon. A few thousand Clevelanders may have an idea that they have seen ball games on the same premises, but those who were not present yesterday will be voted mistaken by those who saw the game. Never in the history of the national game has there been a more sensational finish than the one that the Cleveland team made yesterday, and never before did the same sized audience show as much inclination to go totally insane or give a better oral demonstration of the inclination.

It was a case of hopeless defeat turned into glorious victory. The tide turned at the critical moment, after all hope had been abandoned. A Sheridan in the form of a batting rally arrived from Winchester when Sheridan, Winchester and the batting rally seemed many more than twenty miles away.

Cleveland faced what seemed to be the inevitable in the ninth inning. The spectators had it all figured out how the home team had lost the game. Hoffer had been hit quite freely and his support had been wretched. Four errors were charged to the Cleveland fielders and fourteen hits against the pitcher. Cleveland was only at little matter of eight runs behind, that is, and it required eight runs to tie the score and nine to win when the last half of the ninth began.

The people had left the stands by droves, disgusted with such a one-sided game. The few who remained did so to scoff, but soon stayed to cheer.

Hoffer was the first man up in the ninth and from the bleachers came such sarcastic remarks as:

"Win your own game, Hoffer."

"Hit her out, Hoffer, and run around nine times—then you'll win."

Hoffer struck out. The remainder of the crowd began to start for home when Pickering was thrown out at first. McCarthy sent a clean single to right field and the spectators were offended. It seemed like a useless delay. Bradley hit another one safe and the opinion was that the players were only trying to help their batting averages. But then LaChance, after going after two bad ones, pounded a single to center and McCarthy crossed the plate. Wood was hit by a pitched ball and the bags were full, but even then no one had the slightest hope of pulling the game out of the fire. Scheibeck, however, hit the ball square on the nose for a double. Genins cracked out a single. Patton was taken out of the box and Lee substituted. Egan took four bad ones and Beck, who batted for Hoffer, sent the ball so close to [the] left field fence that Foster could not handle it and the runner took two bases. In the meantime, seven runs had been scored in the inning and one more would tie the game. Pickering singled and Beck went home. By this time the audience gave a life-sized picture of pandemonium let out for recess. A crowd of Indians on a red-hot warpath could not have been more demonstrative.

They roared, they jumped, they shouted. They threw everything within reach in the air. Hats, umbrellas, canes, cushions went up as if a cyclone had struck that part of the landscape. They rushed on the field and came close to losing the game for Cleveland by forfeit.

Pickering's single would have been good for three bases had it not gone into the crowd. The game was stopped until the field was cleared. McCarthy was the man who was given the opportunity of batting in the winning run and he accepted it. A single to left sent Pickering across the plate, he having gone to second on a passed ball.

The demonstration that followed may be imagined— it cannot be described.

The oldest fans fail to recall another similar finish on Cleveland grounds. Once in Boston Cleveland's old Indians won a game by making nine runs off [Jack] Stivetts in the ninth inning and the Fourth of July games in which Philadelphia scored ten runs off Cleveland in the last inning is well remembered here, but on the home grounds the home team never made such a finish before.

The story continued with some standard play-by-play, including the interesting aside that the second baseman Eagan had just arrived from Pittsburgh in apparently a surprise deal.

But the final paragraph was pure poetry.

"Then came Cleveland's ninth inning, which will be remembered until the last person who saw it can remember no more."

Less than 24 years later, on April 14, 1925, under the headline "Indians Down St. Louis, 21 to 14, Browns Make Many Errors, Cleveland Chases 12 Runs Across Plate in Eighth Inning and Turn Impending Defeat Into Victory," Bell offered this dispatch:

St. Louis, MO., April 14—Cleveland's Indians and St. Louis's Browns opened the American League baseball season here this afternoon with a loud detonation. Without the assistance of any lightning calculators *The Plain Dealer* correspondent can only report the score as being 21 to 14 in favor of the Indians. He cannot be held accountable for the accuracy.

The travesty on the well known national pastime, which was put on here was even a burlesque on spring training exhibitions, the climax of some terrible pitching and worse fielding coming in the eighth inning, when the Indians made twelve runs on six hits and five errors by two Brown fielders.

It was not like a major league opening which Clevelanders have been accustomed to. Hundreds of bleachers were empty when the two circuses took to the ring, and thousands of bleacher and grand stand seats were vacant when Joe Shaute, the fifth thrower used by Manager Speaker of the tribe, retired the last man in the ninth.

There was a band, which could not be heard above the din of the crashing bats and the crescendo of jeers for

BIGGEST INNINGS FOR INDIANS

14 runs, June 18, 1950, first inning vs. Philadelphia
13 runs, July 7, 1923, sixth inning vs. Boston
13 runs, April 10, 1977, eighth inning vs. Boston
12 runs, April 14, 1925, eighth inning vs. St. Louis
12 runs, September 10, 1999, fourth inning vs. Chicago
11 runs, August 4, 1996, eighth inning vs. Baltimore

Herschel Bennett and Marty McManus, who made seven errors between them.

The Indians made nineteen hits and the Browns twenty, but the way these two advertised major league organizations slammed the baseball was nothing in comparison to the way in which the remaining St. Louis citizens rose and slammed Philip De Catesby Ball, when the pudgy owner of the Brownies left the stand in the ninth inning.

Mr. Ball, be it known, is the gentleman who was largely responsible for the Indians winning this afternoon. His refusal to give Big Sid Jacobson more than $6,000 per annum for playing center field made it necessary for Herschel Bennett to play that garden this afternoon and Mr. Bennett dropped fly balls like children drop hot potatoes.

Mr. Ball also stood adamant so far in agreeing to the demands of Marty McManus, second baseman, that Marty reported late, with the consequence he was not up to major league infield standards today. He made three errors, which, plus three made by Bennett and four made by Manager George Sisler, gave the home circus ten miscues.

Mr. Ball no doubt felt deeply hurt tonight over the hooting visited upon him this afternoon, but the Indians are for him to a man.

Except for the sandlotting of Bennett and McManus, the tribe would have officiated at this opener as victims instead of victors.

Your correspondent can hardly raise his head tonight in the face of his previous announcements to the effect that Cleveland has a good pitching staff this season. Five of the young men who wear toe plates decorated, or rather desecrated, the rubber, and none showed to particular advantage.

Sherrod Smith started, but the Browns found him for seven runs and nine hits in three and one-third innings.

Byron Speece flipped his underhand stuff for one and two-thirds innings and was nicked for three runs and four hits.

Jim Edwards tried to fool the Brownies with a big curve and after one-third of an inning's toll he gave it up after the ball boosters had score two runs and three hits. Big Boy Buckeye followed him and allowed no runs in one and two-thirds innings, which was the best performance of the afternoon and accounted for him being credited with the victory in the variegated statistics.

Mr. Buckeye was derricked in the eighth for a pinch hitter, or probably Joe Shaute would not have hurled the last two rounds and given the Browns four bases on balls, two doubles and another tally.

Buckeye and Shaute were the only pitchers who fooled the Browns. Shaute would have gone along much better, perhaps, if he hadn't had to sacrifice high powered pitching for accuracy. He frequently had to aim the ball in after getting in the hole.

The way the Indians started off it seemed that they would surely mutilate the Browns, for they made eight runs in the first four innings, but the Browns, after a slow start, scored six tallies in the third and fourth, two in the fifth and four in the sixth.

That gave them an advantage which appeared safe the way Ernest Wingard, the third hurler to be used by Sisler, was going.

But Wingard walked Riggs Stephenson to start the eighth. Then Bennett dropped a fly off the bat of George Burns, who batted for Bob Knode. Before the inning was over, Bennett had dropped another fly and made a wild throw, while McManus booted a grounder and threw one ball high to first.

Sandwiched in between were home runs by Tris Speaker and Patrick McNulty. Other home runs had been made by the Indians before this, one by Jamieson, who opened the game with a fly into the right field stand, and another by Myatt, who lined the sphere into the right center stand in the fourth, but these were not home runs like Speaker's and McNulty's.

Those by Jamieson and Myatt were just punctuation marks in a weird story; those by Speaker and McNulty each came with two runners on base. These gentlemen might be called heroes for knocking in six runs with two hits, but they showed no more puissant form with the stick in that inning than did Chick Fewster, who made two singles, one of which drove in one run and the other, two.

Chick also caught Mr. Wingard asleep and stole third base. All in all, he made himself a noticeable figure during the jubilee.

All told, there were five home runs, for Ken Williams dropped the ball in the right field corner pocket in the fourth, the hit cleaning the bases of two runners. It was from him, perhaps, that Speaker and McNulty got the idea of making home runs with somebody on.

What was McNulty doing in the ball game, anyway? Oh, yes, he ran for Pinch Hitter Uhle in the eighth, and because the side got around to Uhle again, McNulty had to bat.

The home runs accounted for fifteen extra bases, while two two-baggers by the Indians and eight (count 'em, eight) by the Browns, accounted for ten more extra bases, or twenty-five in all.

The play by play account of this unethical opening performance will be found elsewhere and the box score will carry the information that ten pitchers and several pinch hitters, etc., were used, but only a bloomin' idiot could tell you that this was a major league ball game.

RACE RELATIONS

A SHINING EXAMPLE

For all their success, all the championships, and all the great players who have worn the Cleveland uniform, the one thing the Indians really should be known for is their commitment to diversity.

It all started with former owner Bill Veeck, who bought the Indians in the middle of the 1946 season when they were 26–32. Known more as a showman and tireless promoter, Veeck also had a deep commitment to equal rights.

"I have always had a strong feeling for minority groups," Veeck wrote in his autobiography, *Veeck—As in Wreck*, with Ed Linn. "The pat, curbstone explanation would be that having lost a leg myself, I can very easily identify myself with the deprived. Right? Wrong. I had tried to buy the Philadelphia Phillies and stock it with Negro players well before I went into the service.... My only personal experience with discrimination is that I am a left-hander in a right-handed world, a subject on which I can become violent.

"Thinking about it, it seems to me that all my life I have been fighting against the status quo, against the tyranny of the fossilized majority rule. I would suppose that whatever impels me to battle the old fossils of baseball also draws me to the side of the underdog. I would prefer to think of it as an essential decency."

In his autobiography, Veeck continues, "If Jackie Robinson was the ideal man to break the color line, Brooklyn was also the ideal place. I wasn't that sure about Cleveland." Veeck took his time finding the right player. He told his scouts he didn't necessarily want to sign the best player in the Negro Leagues. Rather he wanted to sign the one with the most long-term potential. His choice was Larry Doby.

That Doby would become a baseball pioneer probably never occurred to him as a youngster growing up in the poor Black Bottom section of Camden, South Carolina. Born December 13, 1923, Doby was the son of David Doby, a stablehand who split his time between Camden and Saratoga, and Etta Doby. His parents split up, and his mother went to Paterson, New Jersey, to work as a domestic, leaving her son, nicknamed Bubba, to be raised by her mother, Augusta Brooks. Larry Doby, whose father drowned when Larry was 11, eventually moved in with his aunt and uncle, Alice and James Cookie, and their five children.

Doby attended Jackson School and then Methodist Browning School–Mather Academy in Camden, where he learned to play baseball for Richard DuBose. DuBose remembered Doby's father as a good-hitting first baseman.

When it came time for high school, though, Doby's mother insisted he come to Paterson and attend Eastside High School, a good academic institution that was considered integrated because it had 125 African Americans in its student body of 1,200. Doby became an outstanding athlete at Eastside, earning 11 varsity letters in football, basketball, baseball, and track.

He was every bit as good a basketball player as a baseball player, according to his biographer, Joseph Thomas Moore. In *Pride Against Prejudice: The Biography of Larry Doby*, Moore details how Doby played for the famed Harlem Renaissance pro team that won the National Basketball Tournament in 1938 and also played for the Newark Eagles of the Negro Leagues, using the alias Larry Walker, before he graduated from high school.

At that point, Doby was planning on a career as a physical education teacher and coach. He planned to attend Long Island University and play for legendary basketball coach Clair Bee. But when the United States entered World War II, Doby's plans changed. Instead of LIU, he decided to attend Virginia Union,

Indians team president Bill Veeck gives his newest player, Larry Doby, a big smile at Comiskey Park in Chicago on July 5, 1947, after Doby finished signing a contract with the Indians, making Doby the first black player in the American League.

which had an ROTC program. After helping Virginia Union win its conference championship, he was drafted, wound up in the navy, and was sent to the Pacific atoll Ulithi. That's where he was when he learned of Brooklyn Dodgers owner Branch Rickey's decision to sign Jackie Robinson.

How could Doby know he would be next, and with Cleveland of all places?

When he was honorably discharged in 1946, Doby returned to Newark, married his high school sweetheart, Helyn Curvy, and helped the Eagles win the Negro World Series. By that time, Veeck was already putting his plan to integrate the American League into action.

First, he hired an African American public relations man, Lou Jones, to research the Negro Leagues. In addition to his information gathering, Jones would be able to serve as a companion and confidant to the player selected to join the Indians. Jones recommended Doby, and once Veeck saw that Doby was batting more than .400, Jones didn't have to do much convincing. Veeck paid the Eagles $10,000 to buy Doby's contract. The Indians announced the deal on July 3, 1947, on the eve of that great American holiday—Independence Day.

Doby was 23 when he signed with the Indians in Chicago on July 5, 1947, three months after Robinson broke in with the Dodgers. He was greeted with an ovation from the fans when he walked onto the field, although his arrival in his own clubhouse had not gone quite as smoothly. He also was not allowed to stay with the team in its "whites only" downtown hotel.

Indians manager Lou Boudreau, who did not enjoy the most cordial relationship with Veeck, wrote in his autobiography that he did not know the owner was going to sign Doby and that he feared it was yet another of Veeck's publicity stunts.

According to Moore, Doby's biographer, Boudreau issued a statement that read, "The acquisition of Larry Doby, an infielder formerly with the Newark Eagles team, is a routine baseball purchase in my mind. Creed, race, or color are not factors in baseball success, whether it be in the major or minor leagues. Ability and character are the only factors. Doby will be given every chance, as will any other deserving recruit, to prove that he has the ability to make good with us. The reports we have received on his ability are outstanding. I hope that he can succeed with us as he has with other teams."

DID YOU KNOW...

That the Indians brought in more players from the Negro Leagues than any other major league team? According to the team's press guide, which cites *The Negro Leagues Book*, 15 former Negro Leaguers joined the Indians: Walt Bond, Joe Caffie, Larry Doby, Luke Easter, Billy Harrell, Dave Hoskins, Sam Jones, Minnie Minoso, Satchel Paige, Dave Pope, Larry Raines, Jose Santiago, Harry Simpson, Al Smith, and Quincy Trouppe.

On the day of Doby's signing, Boudreau introduced Doby around the clubhouse. Two players reportedly refused to shake his hand—Les Fleming and Eddie Robinson. Robinson also reportedly refused to lend Doby a glove, although Robinson later insisted that he was worried about his spot on the team and not about the color of Doby's skin.

At any rate, Boudreau and Doby walked to the field together and began to play catch before the game. In the seventh inning, Boudreau inserted Doby as a pinch hitter, but he struck out, returning to the bench and putting his head in his hands. Indians lore has teammate Joe Gordon also striking out and then sitting down next to Doby on the bench and putting his head in his hands, too. That would be a great story if it were true. But the fact of the matter is that Gordon had walked to start the inning and was on third base when Doby struck out.

The rest of the weekend passed uneventfully, with Doby making his first start in the field at first base in the second game of a doubleheader the next day.

The media responded positively to Doby's debut.

Wrote Cleveland Jackson in the *Call and Post* newspaper, "For Larry Doby, it took but a few short minutes to walk up to that plate. But for 13 million American Negroes, that simple action was the successful climax of a long, uphill fight whose annals are like the saga of the [black] race."

In *The Plain Dealer*, Gordon Cobbledick referred to the 6'1", 180-pound Doby as "the coppery-skinned colored boy" but wrote, "People are doing a lot of unnecessary guessing as to how Larry Doby, the Indians' newest rookie, will be accepted by his teammates and by the customers. He will be accepted by both groups if he proves to be a good ballplayer and a good human being and will be rejected by both if the opposite is true. How do I know? Well, the Cleveland Browns of the All-American Football Conference signed two Negro players last year to the deep consternation of their rival teams. There had been no colored boys in the white professional leagues, and it was evident that all except the Browns intended to keep it that way if possible. Today, something less than a year later, every team in the All-America Conference is beating the bushes in a desperate effort to find a good Negro football player or two—another Bill Willis or another Marion Motley."

Cobbledick's choice of words might make modern readers cringe, but no one reacted that way in 1947. Furthermore, he proved to be prophetic. And, as a matter of fact, Browns stars Willis and Motley were among those who greeted Doby when he stepped off the train upon the team's arrival in Cleveland from Chicago on July 8, 1947. An article in that day's *Plain Dealer* gave a candid glimpse into what Doby had been feeling during his debut. "When I first went to bat in Chicago, I was so scared I didn't even know how many men were out, and all I had to do was look at the scoreboard. I never did swing at a strike. I was so tense at the plate. It all seems like a dream now."

The rest of his first season was more like a nightmare. On the field, he went a dismal (and totally uncharacteristic) 5 for 32, .156. And while he had the full support of Veeck and teammates like Gordon and Jim Hegan, among others, he still often could not stay or have dinner with the rest of his teammates. In a 2001 interview with *Plain Dealer* reporter Bob Dolgan, Doby said, "It was one of the toughest things I ever had to go through."

Things actually got worse—at least temporarily—before they got better. After the season, the Indians told Doby he likely wouldn't be able to unseat Gordon at second base and suggested he learn how to play the outfield. So during the off-season, Doby read the book, *How to Play the Outfield*, by Tommy Henrich of the New York Yankees. During spring training, he got some more pointers from former Indians star and manager Tris Speaker. He picked up enough to make the team as a right fielder, and when Thurman Tucker got hurt, he moved into center field, where he played the next eight seasons, making seven All-Star teams.

Doby helped the Indians win the 1948 World Series after that season and made a lasting impression on race relations in this country. Literally. Doby and pitcher Steve Gromek were featured in a photograph after the Indians took a 3–1 lead in the best-of-seven World Series against the Boston Braves. Doby's home run gave Gromek and the Indians a 2–1 victory on October 9. In the photo, Gromek is hugging Doby and the two smiling ballplayers

---

HAPPY BIRTHDAY TO SATCHEL

No one has ever been sure of Satchel Paige's age, and Paige loved keeping the secret. When he joined the Indians in 1948, he was in his forties, but how far into his forties no one was quite sure—including owner Bill Veeck.

Veeck did take some pains to find out, though, going right to the source as he wrote in his autobiography, *Veeck—As in Wreck*.

"After a great deal of difficulty, I was able to reach Mrs. Paige at her local general store in Mobile, Alabama, which had the only phone in the neighborhood. I found out quickly enough the source of Satch's humor. 'I can't rightly recall whether Leroy was my firstborn,' she said, 'or my fifteenth.' Having had her joke, she told me she really couldn't remember what year he had been born, but that she could guarantee he wasn't her oldest.

"Well, it was a start. I hired a private detective to check the birth records at the city hall in Mobile. Here's what he reported: the Mobile records did not go back any farther than mid-1900, and while there was no record of Satch himself, one of his younger brothers was on the 1901 list.... This could only mean, then, that Satch could not possibly have been born any later than the early part of 1900. Satch himself always gave his birthday as September 18. Assuming that a man has a sentimental attachment to his actual birthday, Satch could not have been born any later than September 18, 1899."

---

are cheek-to-cheek. Nowadays, no one would even notice. But baseball had been integrated only two years at that point, and there weren't a lot of photographs that showed black and white players in similar fashion.

In fact, when sportswriter Bob Dolgan interviewed Doby for a series on the 50th anniversary of that 1948 World Series, Doby told Dolgan that photograph was his personal World Series highlight.

"It was an emotional time," Doby told Dolgan, who also used the story in his book *Heroes, Scamps, and Good Guys.* "We had won and we showed respect for each other. The picture showed that black and white people could get along and work together. I don't think too many people were ready for that type of picture in '48."

Dolgan also interviewed Gromek, who told him, "Color was never an issue with me. Doby won the game for me. I was happy. I always got along with him. He won a lot of games for me with his bat and glove."

Doby hit a career-high .326 in 1950, when he was named the Indians' Man of the Year. In 1952, he led the AL with 32 home runs. In 1954, he led the league with 32 home runs and 126 RBIs as the Indians won the pennant before being swept by the New York Giants in the World Series.

The Indians traded Doby to the Chicago White Sox for short-stop Chico Carrasquel and center fielder Jim Busby on October 25, 1955, but got him back from Baltimore in a trade on April 1, 1958. On May 13, 1959, the Indians traded him again, this time to Detroit for Tito Francona. He retired after that season. The Indians retired his No. 14 on July 3, 1994. In his major league career, Doby batted .283 with 253 home runs. He was elected to the Baseball Hall of Fame in 1998 and died of cancer on June 18, 2003. He was 79. At the time of his death, former Indians teammate Bob Feller likened Doby to astronaut Buzz Aldrin, the second man on the moon, because he was the second black player in the major leagues.

"I'm happy with the career I had," Doby once told *The Plain Dealer*. Asked if he resented any of the slights he endured, he said, "Life is too short for that. People who judge others based on the color of their skin have more problems than I do."

After retiring from Major League Baseball, Doby played in Japan and then became a scout and batting coach for Montreal and a first-base coach for the Indians before managing the Chicago White Sox. Oddly enough, he was passed over when Indians owner Nick Mileti and general manager Phil Seghi made Frank Robinson the first African American manager in baseball history on October 3, 1974.

Doby was disappointed, to be sure, but said, "I am happy that baseball is now showing it's not prejudiced.... I'm sure Jackie Robinson will be smiling when Robby is hired, because he's the reason it's all happening now."

A MONUMENTAL MOVE

Almost 20 years after Jackie Robinson and Larry Doby became the first African American players in baseball, Frank Robinson—no relation to Jackie Robinson—became the first African American manager when he took over the Indians.

On that historic occasion, Rachel Robinson, Jackie's widow, told reporters, "I think it would have been one of Jackie's biggest thrills. He would have been ecstatic. Things didn't have to involve him personally for him to be excited."

Baseball commissioner Bowie Kuhn and American League president Lee MacPhail flew to Cleveland for Frank Robinson's press conference. More than 100 reporters were present. Imagine what it might draw today with ESPN and the Internet.

Robinson, who had joined the Indians as a player late in the 1974 season, tried to downplay the historical significance of becoming the first black manager.

Frank Robinson speaks at a news conference after being named the major leagues' first black manager on October 3, 1974.

"I'm the first one only because I was born black," he said.

Said Seghi, "Frank Robinson is here because he has all the qualities we've been searching for. I felt I wanted Frank because I wanted the very best man available. I had no reservations whatsoever about hiring him."

Asked about the potential problem of becoming the first black manager to be fired, Robinson said, "I don't see any problem in firing me or any black manager. If I'm not doing the job, I should be fired. And if I don't do the job and I'm fired, I don't think there'll be any real repercussions."

Robinson did use his appointment to praise baseball's pioneer.

"I don't know if I could go through what Jackie went through, and I thank the Lord for making him the kind of man he was," Robinson said. "If I had only one wish that could be answered, it would be that Jackie Robinson could be here today."

If there was any grumbling about Frank Robinson's appointment, and there probably was in some circles, it was kept quiet. Instead, all the public reaction was positive.

As sports editor Hal Lebovitz wrote in *The Plain Dealer*, "Frank Robinson is a man whose time has come and who is entitled to the opportunity to which he has dedicated himself.... Because he is the first, there will be much made of the color of his skin in all the dispatches and tapes and films. As we wrote Sunday, he will be the first black manager at the start of the season—perhaps the first half—but after that, he'll no longer be unique. He'll simply become Frank Robinson, Manager. And he'll rise or fall, not on the color of his skin but on his ability, or lack of it, to handle pitchers; on his ability, or lack of it, to run a ballclub.... personally I'm glad to see he is getting the opportunity.

TRIVIA

If Frank Robinson was the first African American manager in Major League Baseball, who was the second?

Find the answers on pages 159–160.

"I would rather have a fresh, eager, deserving Robinson than some washed-out manager who has made the rounds. It's another exciting adventure in Cleveland baseball history, and I'm glad to be aboard for the ride. I hope all the fans look at it this way.... He is a man whose time has come and who has been given the opportunity. I wish him the very best. I hope every Indians fan does."

Bill Veeck, the owner who had signed Doby as a player, was disappointed Doby wasn't hired but said, "I'm delighted somebody is finally becoming intelligent enough to select a manager on ability rather than his color. I'm glad to find a club where an unknown doesn't frighten them to death. That is the only reason for the hesitancy in hiring a black manager."

Said Earl Weaver, who managed Robinson in Baltimore, "Frank is definitely ready to be a major league manager. I hope people judge him on his merits, not whether he is white or black. There is no doubt in my mind that he will do a good job."

Indians players also voiced their support.

"I think it's a hell of a move for black people," said first baseman/outfielder Tom McCraw. "This compares to Jackie Robinson and Larry Doby getting their chances to play in the big leagues. But it's also a good move for the Cleveland club. Nobody around here cares what color he is, and I have no doubt Frank will do a good job."

Said pitcher Dick Bosman, "If he manages the way he played—he'll do anything to beat you—I'm sure I'm going to like him very much."

Added pitcher Tom Buskey, "It doesn't make any difference if he's black or white. Not to me it doesn't. I don't particularly like the idea of him trying to be a designated hitter and manager, because I think managing required 100 percent concentration. But maybe he is capable of doing both."

It took only one game for Robinson to prove that.

On Opening Day, April 8, 1975, Robinson hit a two-run home run in his first at-bat to help the Indians to a 5–3 victory over the visiting New York Yankees. It was the 575th home run in Robinson's 20-year career—but his first as a manager.

"Any home run is a thrill, but I've got to admit, this one was a bigger thrill," Robinson told reporters after the game. "Right now I feel better than I have after anything I've done in this game.

Take all the pennants, the personal awards, the World Series, the All-Star Games together and this moment is the greatest."

In spite of a temperature of 36 degrees, a crowd of 56,204 took in the game. Wrote Lebovitz, "Even if you were frozen, the heart pounded faster and the blood flowed quicker from the thrill." The headline on his column asked, "Was it fiction...?"

The top headline on the front page of *The Plain Dealer* that day referred to Robinson's storybook debut, and Russell Schneider wrote, "It was the kind of a debut for Robinson that even Hollywood wouldn't dare manufacture."

Though the day belonged to Robinson, his co-star might have been pitcher Gaylord Perry, the Cy Young Award winner in 1972. After Robinson was hired, Perry was quoted as saying he'd demand $1 more in salary and the two clashed in spring training over Perry's attitude. Yet after Perry threw the first pitch on that Opening Day, he tossed the baseball to Robinson in the dugout as a memento of the historic occasion. After Robinson's home run, Perry led his teammates out to greet Robinson at the plate.

It was quite a debut for a young man born August 31, 1935, in Silsbee, Texas, the youngest of 10 children. His parents split up, and some of the children, including little Frank, moved with their mother to Oakland, California, where Robinson grew up and became a star athlete at McClymonds High School under coach (and father figure) George Powles. Robinson was just 17 when he was signed by Cincinnati. He played one year in Ogden, Utah, batting .348 with 17 home runs and 83 RBIs, before moving to Tulsa and then Columbia, South Carolina. Under manager Birdie Tebbetts in Cincinnati, Robinson hit .290 with 38 home runs and 83 RBIs and was the 1956 National League Rookie of the Year. In 1961, he hit .323 with 37 home runs and 124 RBIs, led the Reds to the NL pennant, and was named the NL MVP. After being traded to Baltimore in 1965, he won the 1966 Triple Crown—batting .316 with 49 home runs and 122 RBIs—and was named the AL MVP. He was traded to the Los Angeles Dodgers in 1971 and to the California Angels in 1972. Two years later, the Indians obtained the 11-time All-Star as a player and by the end of the season, they'd chosen him to lead the team as the first black manager in history.

FELLOW PIONEERS

The first African American pro football coach was Fritz Pollard with the Akron Pros/Indians of the American Professional Football League (later renamed the National Football League) in 1921.

The first African American pro basketball coach was John McLendon with the Cleveland Pipers of the American Basketball League in 1961. Bill Russell was the first African American to coach in the National Basketball Association with the Boston Celtics in 1966.

Like anyone new to a job, Robinson found he had a lot to learn.

"More and more I'm realizing that managing doesn't involve just baseball," he wrote in a book on his first season that he co-authored with Dave Anderson titled *Frank: The First Year*.

The Indians finished that season 79–80, their best record in seven years.

"I always did what I thought was right, what I thought was best for the team," Robinson said. "I have no regrets, and if I had things to do all over again, I'd do everything the same way. I'm looking forward to the day when people will stop writing, 'Frank Robinson, baseball's first black manager,' and just write, 'Frank Robinson, manager of the Cleveland Indians.'"

In 1976, the Indians improved to 81–78, the first time they'd finished better than .500 since 1968. But when they got off to a 26–31 start in 1977, Robinson was fired on June 19, becoming the first black manager to be fired.

"I'm not upset; disappointed is a better way to say it," he said. "It's almost like they're telling me I failed, and I don't believe I failed in anything."

Indeed, Robinson, who was elected to the Baseball Hall of Fame in 1982, went on to manage the San Francisco Giants, the Baltimore Orioles, the Montreal Expos, and the Washington Nationals. He was named Manager of the Year in 1989, when he led Baltimore to an 87–75 record after the Orioles lost 101 games in 1988.

ANOTHER HISTORIC DEBUT

Before Jackie Robinson, before Larry Doby, before Frank Robinson, there was Louis Francis Sockalexis.

Sockalexis, a Penobscot Indian born October 24, 1871, outside Old Town, Maine, is generally considered the first full-blooded Native American to play major league baseball, competing for the Cleveland Spiders from 1897–99. Research has revealed that James Madison Toy, who was half Sioux and half Caucasian, played in the American Association in 1887 and 1890, although it is unclear whether anyone was aware of his Native American heritage.

There was no doubt about Sockalexis's heritage. In fact, at least two books have been written about his life, and both identify him as the first Native American to play Major League Baseball. In the Indians press guide, Sockalexis's debut season in 1897 is compared to that of Jackie Robinson and Doby 50 years later "as a landmark campaign featuring an athlete attempting to hurdle prejudice to succeed."

Sockalexis's life certainly makes good reading. He was a gifted natural athlete, and tales of his prowess abound. Witnesses recall him throwing a baseball 600 feet across the Penobscot River. He played at Holy Cross, where he batted .440 in two seasons and stole six bases in one game. He also ran track and played football. He transferred to the University of Notre Dame, but was expelled after a drinking incident. He reported to Cleveland amid much fanfare and attracted legions of fans—many of them female.

As Brian McDonald wrote in *Indian Summer: The Forgotten Story of Louis Francis Sockalexis, The First Native American in Major League Baseball*, "Dwarfing his teammates at nearly six feet and 190 pounds, solid as Carnegie steel, Sockalexis filled out every stitch of his uniform, not like the other scrawny players with their baggy uniform pants. His hair was raven-black to his shoulders. Where most of the players then had droopy mustaches, the Indian's face was smooth as a sophomore's, his complexion like deep-red wine." According to McDonald, Sockalexis's clothes were tailor-made, and he often came to the ballpark with a sweater knotted around his shoulders.

Yet in spite of his pleasing appearance, and his skill at the plate and in the outfield, he was subjected to taunts and war-whoops every time he came to bat. But if he was bothered by them, he never showed it. In 66 games in his first season, he batted .338 (94 of 278) with 42 RBIs. Surely the highlight of his career was the home run he hit out of the Polo Grounds off star pitcher Amos Rusie of the New York Giants that first season. The sad part is that Sockalexis's career lasted just 28 more games, 21 the next season and seven in 1899. His drinking was his downfall.

He returned to Maine, where he taught youngsters on the reservation to play baseball. He died of a heart attack in 1913 at the age of 42, reportedly carrying yellowed newspaper clippings from his days as a baseball player. Two years later, the Cleveland baseball team took the name Indians.

There has been much debate over whether that was a tribute to Sockalexis or a convenient out when the nickname and Chief Wahoo logo were criticized.

That the team was in need of a new nickname was not in question. To that point, the Cleveland baseball team had been called, in order, the Forest Citys, the Spiders, the Bluebirds (short-ened to Blues), the Bronchos, and the Naps, in honor of star player-manager Napoleon Lajoie, who departed after the 1914 season.

For years, it was believed a poll of newspaper readers selected "Indians" in honor of Sockalexis. But research by sportswriter Bob

LOUIS SOCKALEXIS'S BATTING AVERAGE BY SEASONS

1897 94 for 278 .338 in 66 games
1898 15 for 67 .224 in 21 games
1899 6 for 22 .273 in 7 games

Dolgan of *The Plain Dealer* found that while fans were asked to send in suggestions for a new name, there was no official contest and Sockalexis was barely mentioned in stories about the new name. Instead, owner Charles Somers apparently solicited suggestions from the baseball writers, who reportedly polled their readers, and Indians was selected. The team occasionally had been referred to as the Indians whenever Sockalexis had a good game, but Dolgan's research and that of others indicated the nickname was used derisively as well.

In response, the Indians began including in their press guides a passage from a story published in *The Plain Dealer* on January 18, 1915, dealing with the new nickname. It read, "Many years ago, there was an Indian named Sockalexis who was the star of the Cleveland baseball club. As batter, fielder, and base runner he was a marvel. Sockalexis so far outshone his teammates that he naturally came to be regarded as the whole team. The fans throughout the country began to call the Clevelanders the 'Indians.' It was an honorable name, and while it stuck the team made an excellent record.

"It now has been decided to revive this name. The Cleveland of 1915 will be the 'Indians.' There will be no real Indians on the roster, but the name will recall fine traditions. It is looking backward to a time when Cleveland had one of the most popular teams of the United States. It also serves to revive the memory of a single great player who has been gathered to his fathers in the happy hunting ground of Abenakis."

TAKE THIS JOB AND SHOVE IT

A MAN OF MYSTERY

Moe Berg wasn't an Indian for long, just parts of two seasons. In his professional career, he had much longer stints with the Chicago White Sox and the Boston Red Sox, and he also played for the Brooklyn Dodgers and Washington Senators.

A lot of players kicked around more than he did. A lot lasted much longer. Even more didn't last as long. But what made him stand apart from all those players who preceded and succeeded him was that Berg also served as a spy for the United States government. Talk about going to the opposite field.

He may have been the most intriguing athlete ever to play Major League Baseball, much less for the Indians.

The seeds for this unusual career were sown in his childhood. Berg was born March 2, 1902, in New York City, the second son of Bernard and Rose Berg, Ukrainian immigrants. Bernard Berg held a series of jobs in New York before he and his wife opened a laundry. Then Bernard studied to become a pharmacist and relocated his family to Newark, where he opened a drug store. A man who had a gift for languages, he always spoke to his customers in their own languages.

Such a skill was not lost on young Moe. For most of his life he was able to pursue his love of languages and his love of baseball. By the age of seven, he already had demonstrated a considerable talent for baseball, and he became a star third baseman at

Former Indians player and erudite, spy, linguist, and world traveler Morris (Moe) Berg in a 1970 photo.

Barringer High School. He attended New York University before transferring to Princeton, where he became the varsity shortstop while studying languages. He was fluent in Italian, French, German, Spanish, Latin, and even Sanskrit, and graduated magna cum laude.

Recognized as something of a loner and a man of mystery even back then, Berg's college career was not a totally happy one. According to the book *Moe Berg: Athlete, Scholar, Spy* by Louis Kaufman, Barbara Fitzgerald, and Tom Sewell, Berg encountered some anti-semitism in the school's social clubs, which played a part in the fact that he never returned to the campus for reunions. Of course, as he grew older he also grew more reclusive, which played a part as well.

At any rate, after graduation in 1923, he turned down an offer to teach in the language department at Princeton and signed with the Brooklyn Robins for $5,000. He played shortstop back then and batted just .186 in 49 games.

After the season, he attended the Sorbonne to further his study of languages, but he returned in time for the 1924 baseball season. He played for Minneapolis and Toledo in the American Association, batting .264. In 1925, he moved up to the International League, where he batted .311 in Reading.

In 1926, the White Sox bought his contract from Reading for $50,000. He played in 41 games with a fairly anemic batting average of .221. In August of the following season, he switched to catcher when a rash of injuries left the White Sox without one. He'd caught one game in high school, which meant he had more experience behind the plate than the rest of his teammates. In his first game at catcher, the White Sox lost to Boston, 4–1, but the Red Sox only stole one base. It was a strong enough performance to prompt a position change, which probably prolonged his major league career given that catchers are tougher to come by than infielders. At any rate, his most productive season came in 1929, when he batted .287 in 107 games for the White Sox.

In 1930, he ruptured ligaments in his right knee during spring training and later developed pneumonia. As a result, he played only 20 games and batted just .115. In 1931, he was sold to the Indians but played only 10 games, with one hit in 13 at-bats, a .077 batting average. He was released after that season and signed by Washington. In 1932, his career revived a bit. He caught 75 games and hit .236 for the Senators.

Partly as a result of his athletic resurgence, he became a popular party guest around town, especially at some of the many embassies that made up so much of the Washington, D.C., social scene. In addition to his athletic prowess and his facility for languages, he had graduated from Columbia Law School and practiced law in the off-season at a Wall Street firm by the name of Satterlee and Canfield. An avid newspaper reader who was well-versed on almost any subject, Berg also had begun to study military history, another popular subject in Washington. (His many and varied interests led sportswriters to call him "The Professor," a nickname he did not care for at all.)

It was after the 1932 season that Berg made what is believed to be his first trip to Japan. He had become fascinated with the country and learned how to speak the language. He conducted a baseball clinic there and then took an incredibly circuitous route home, visiting Korea, China, India, Cambodia, Arabia, Palestine, Jerusalem, Bethlehem, Nazareth, and Athens, among other places. He made his second trip in October 1934, after splitting his season between Washington and Cleveland. This time, he was part of a U.S. team that included Indians teammate Earl Averill, as well as Babe Ruth, Lou Gehrig, Jimmie Foxx, Lefty Gomez, and manager Connie Mack. The team of stars was scheduled to play some exhibition games, and the players were mobbed by fans wherever they went. In one park, the fans reportedly cheered for four minutes after Ruth hit a home run.

The fascinating book on Berg by Kaufman, Fitzgerald, and Sewell opens with that trip to Japan and the fact that, unlike the rest of those in the traveling party, Berg was carrying a letter addressed to American diplomatic and consular officers and signed by Secretary of State Cordell Hull that advised them of his arrival in Japan.

"He certainly didn't let on to anything," said Tigers Hall of Famer Charlie Gehringer, who was on the trip. "I didn't know how involved he was in things. I didn't have any State Department letter from Secretary Hull and I didn't realize that Moe did. I know of no other players who took the trip that had one either. My other recollection of Moe on that trip is that of correcting some of the Japanese fellows on their grammar."

During the tour, Berg skipped a game, snuck into St. Luke's International Hospital on the pretense of visiting the U.S. ambassador's wife, who had given birth to a baby girl, made his way to the roof, and took films of Tokyo that were later used in air raids during World War II.

"I never really saw Moe Berg," Elizabeth Lyon told the authors. "It was an extraordinary occurrence. Moe came with the pretext of visiting me. Despite heavy screening at the hospital, he apparently said he had come to visit the ambassador's daughter, got on an elevator, and kept on going, somehow, to the hospital roof. Yes, I was his excuse. My daughter Alice Emily's birth was noted in Tokyo papers and that is where Moe most likely learned of it. St. Luke's was a very modern hospital and a skyscraper by Tokyo standards. I was on the sixth or seventh floor, I think. But Moe never entered my room. It was some time later that I was first told of the incident. The pictures taken by Moe Berg at the hospital were used in the General [Jimmy] Doolittle raid during the war."

Berg told no one where he'd been, and he tried to brush off questions about his absence by telling teammates he didn't feel well. That didn't sit quite right for two reasons: one, he'd never been one to miss games for health reasons, and two, he didn't tell anyone he wasn't feeling well beforehand. Even if his traveling companions were willing to accept one absence, they couldn't help but notice that he missed a number of other social engagements as well.

The authors talked to a number of people who'd been on the trip.

"It wasn't until years later that I learned Moe was a spy," Averill told them. "I didn't know it at the time. He was the right man, of course. Moe had the guts of a cat burglar."

Said Yankee pitcher Gomez, "Moe was a mysterious guy all his life. He looked the same at six in the morning, eight in the evening, or at midnight. He was always moving about. He was always coming from some place or other. No one ever knew where he lived or what he did with his time. He'd spend some time with the guys but overall Moe Berg was a total mystery. You could

---

DID YOU KNOW...

That Moe Berg's father wouldn't watch him play professional baseball because he was disappointed his son hadn't become a lawyer or doctor? One can only wonder if part of Berg's pursuit of knowledge and his clandestine career weren't an effort to win the approval of his very intelligent and patriotic father.

expect anything as far as Moe was concerned. But being missing from the ballpark is something else again. He wasn't scheduled to catch that day, but he should have been in uniform in the bullpen ready to warm pitchers up or play if necessary. But the game, of course, went on without Moe."

Added June Gomez, "I remember Moe did an awful lot of traveling in Japan. He took a lot of trips where other ballplayers and the rest of us did not go. We thought it unusual that Moe failed to take some of the scheduled socializing trips. He was always going off somewhere alone. But Moe was so pleasant on the trip and we all enjoyed him immensely. He was just different, that's all."

After the trip, Berg stayed in Japan for two weeks and then did some more traveling, including a ride on the Trans-Siberian Railroad. He returned to the Red Sox for the 1935 season, playing in 38 games and batting .286. His average dipped to .240 in 1936, when he played in 39 games.

Lefty Gomez recalled preparing for a game against the Red Sox in 1936 when Berg approached him in the bullpen and asked about some photos Gomez had taken in Japan, particularly those of Yokohama Harbor. Berg pressed Gomez about the pictures and asked if Gomez would send the film to an address in Washington, D.C.

"I mailed the film to Washington," Gomez told the authors. "I don't know specifically who received them. They kept it for seven or eight months and then it was returned with a letter that expressed thanks. I never mentioned the incident. My camera was a 16-mm Stewart Warner and it could film for quite a distance if it was set for it."

By this time, baseball players and others were wondering about Berg's secret life. There were rumors he was a spy. Eventually a report in *The New York Times* said Berg had posed as a Swiss businessman in order to track down Germany's atomic secrets. Gomez always figured it was none of his business, even when he and some other players on a goodwill trip to visit U.S. soldiers in Naples during World War II ran into Berg and he wouldn't speak to them.

"I never had any indication that my brother was a spy while a ballplayer but I'm not surprised that he agreed to carry out these missions," Berg's brother, Samuel, told the authors. "Moe was from an era and background that held strong loyalties to the country. Our parents were fiercely loyal and proud of America. This trait was reflected in Moe, I feel, when the government made requests of him. I'm sure that he was flattered that the government asked him to serve."

Said Red Sox owner Tom Yawkey, "I had no evidence that Moe Berg was a spy while with the Red Sox. Why, it would be inconceivable. But it would surprise me, knowing what I know now, if he hadn't engaged in some form of espionage during his tenure with us. You'd think he would drop a hint to those close to him, but he never let on. He never said anything to anybody. But that was Moe. No man came more decent, more mysterious or more secretive."

Berg retired from baseball on June 14, 1941. Sadly, it was the same day his father died.

About the same time, Berg began work with the Office of the Coordinator of Inter-American Affairs (CIAA) headed by Nelson Rockefeller. Berg was named a goodwill ambassador to Latin America. In addition to trying to improve relations between that part of the world and the United States, he also did a lot of research of political figures in order to assess their sympathies with regard to the United States.

After the Japanese bombed Pearl Harbor on December 7, 1941, Berg delivered an impassioned radio broadcast—in Japanese—asking the Japanese to put down their arms. Whereas the Japanese had cheered the American baseball heroes seven years earlier, shortly after Berg's radio address the Japanese banned baseball for a time.

The Office of the Coordinator of Information became the Office of Strategic Services (OSS) in 1942, and Berg joined the agency, the precursor to the CIA, on August 1, 1943. From this point on, some of the tales recounted in the book *Moe Berg: Athlete, Scholar, Spy* sound as if they came out of a James Bond script. But they're true and, as the authors discovered through

MOE BERG YEAR-BY-YEAR

Year	Team	G	AB	R	H	2B	3B	HR	RBI	SB	CS	BB	SO	BA
1923	BRO	49	129	9	24	3	0	0	6	1	0	2	5	.186
1926	CHW	41	113	4	25	6	0	0	7	0	2	6	9	.221
1927	CHW	35	69	4	17	4	0	0	4	0	0	4	10	.246
1928	CHW	76	224	25	55	16	0	0	29	2	1	14	25	.246
1929	CHW	107	352	32	101	7	0	0	47	5	1	17	16	.287
1930	CHW	20	61	4	7	3	0	0	7	0	0	1	5	.115
1931	CLE	10	13	1	1	1	0	0	0	0	0	1	1	.077
1932	WSH	75	195	16	46	8	1	0	26	1	1	8	13	.236
1933	WSH	40	65	8	12	3	0	2	9	0	0	4	5	.185
1934	TOT	62	183	9	46	7	0	0	15	2	0	7	11	.251
	WSH	33	86	5	21	4	0	0	6	2	0	6	4	.244
	CLE	29	97	4	25	3	0	0	9	0	0	1	7	.258
1935	BOS	38	98	13	28	5	1	2	12	0	0	5	3	.286
1936	BOS	39	125	9	30	4	0	0	19	0	0	2	6	.240
1937	BOS	47	141	13	36	3	1	0	20	0	0	5	4	.255
1938	BOS	10	12	0	4	0	0	0	0	0	0	0	1	.333
1939	BOS	14	33	3	9	1	0	0	0	0	0	2	3.	.314
15 years		663	1813	150	441	71	6	6	206	11	5	78	117	.243

research and interviews, Berg was America's premier atomic spy during World War II, focusing on Germany's atomic, biological, and chemical warfare, as well as Nazi war crimes.

Berg's first OSS assignment was to go to Yugoslavia to assess its rival armies and advise the United States on which one to support. He traveled to Norway to check the status of a heavy water plant that had been sabotaged. He once masqueraded as a German officer in a munitions plant in Florence. He became obsessed with finding Herr Professor Werner Heisenberg, Germany's foremost atomic scientist, and eventually provided information that led to his capture. As a result, Berg was nominated for the Medal of Merit, the highest honor for a civilian during wartime. He respectfully refused the award without explanation.

After World War II, Berg spied on the Russians for a short time, but resigned on October 19, 1946.

He moved in with his brother, but he was not easy to live with. As always, he was a voracious reader, and newspapers littered the house. He never wanted anyone to touch them, believing they were alive until he read them. Such habits would make him a difficult roommate.

Berg died May 30, 1972, at the age of 70. He never talked about his adventures.

CALLING DR. HARDY

Giovanni Berardino was born in Los Angeles. It was almost as if he was destined to become an actor.

But before he changed his name to John Beradino and became fatherly Dr. Steve Hardy, the undisputed patriarch of the long-running ABC soap opera *General Hospital*, Berardino was a baseball player.

Born May 1, 1917, Berardino grew to be a 6', 180-pound infielder at the University of Southern California for coach Sam Barry. He was signed as an amateur free agent by the St. Louis Browns in 1937 and made his major league debut on April 22, 1939. He started out batting .256 his rookie year and hit 16 home runs the following season. In 1941, he batted .258 and drove in

89 runs, then hit .284 in 29 games in 1942 before taking a three-year hiatus in the armed forces during World War II. He batted .265 in 1946 and .261 in 1947 before being traded to Cleveland for Catfish Metkovich and $50,000 on December 9, 1947. (Metkovich was found to have a broken finger, so he was returned to the Indians, who sent an additional $15,000 to the Browns.)

According to then-owner Bill Veeck, in *Veeck—As in Wreck*, there was some "acting" going on in his negotiations with his new utility infielder.

The most fun I ever had in a publicity holdout was with Johnny Berardino, a utility infielder I had bought from St. Louis for $50,000, for reasons I will go into slowly. John had landed a couple of bit parts in the movies, hired an agent and, in order that his acting career would not go completely unnoticed, had been threatening to quit baseball and devote himself to his art.

So when I bought Berardino I got myself a built-in publicity gimmick to fool around with. John announced that he was going to bring his agent along to negotiate his baseball contract for him, another first in the wonderful world of sports.

John is a delightful fellow and we had some very pleasant conversations for about a week, although the agent, who suffered under some strange delusion that we were really there to talk contract, proved to be a distracting influence. Especially after he got carried away by all the publicity and seemed to think he had to justify his presence by talking in upper-bracket figures.

I knew what I was going to pay John, John knew I knew what I was going to pay him. I mean that agent never got into the spirit of a contract negotiation at all....

Finally, I told John: "I think we've pushed this about as far as it will go. We'd better sign something."

John turned to his agent and said, "All right, you better leave now. You're not very practical and you'll end up getting Bill so mad that you'll cost me money."

Just to keep the gag going, we thought it prudent to protect John's future by taking out an insurance policy on his face. If Johnny Berardino had been hit on the face by a batted ball that year and left so disfigured that he was no longer able to pursue his career as an actor, he would have been compensated to the amount of one million dollars. This policy cost me something like 78 cents a month (I was covering him both home and away) but, as I always say, nothing is too good for one of my boys.

Having, through incredible good fortune, preserved his features, Berardino has gone on to a fairly successful acting career. You see him on television all the time now. For a while, I always seemed to see him being gunned down by one of Al Capone's boys—for this, I had to protect his features?—although he has now straightened himself out and has been rewarded with the second lead in *The New Breed*.

Although Veeck made fun of the negotiations, Berardino was no joke. He batted just .190 in 66 games in 1948, but he was an important asset to the Indians' drive to the World Series championship that season because he was reportedly the team's best bench jockey and he could play all three infield positions. In fact, in his major league career, which spanned 11 seasons with St. Louis, Cleveland, and Pittsburgh, he played first base, second base, third base, shortstop, and the outfield. His career with the Indians lasted until 1950, when the team sent him down to the minor leagues and then released him. He played a short time for Pittsburgh in 1950, and returned to St. Louis in 1951. In 1952 he was back with the Indians. After playing 35 games and batting

DID YOU KNOW...

That John Berardino was so beloved that photos of him remained in the opening sequence of *General Hospital* until 2004, eight years after his death?

JOHN BERARDINO YEAR-BY-YEAR

Year	Team	G	AB	R	H	2B	3B	HR	RBI	SB	CS	BB	SO	BA
1939	SLB	126	468	42	120	24	5	5	58	6	2	37	36	.256
1940	SLB	142	523	71	135	31	4	16	85	6	8	32	46	.258
1941	SLB	128	469	48	127	30	4	5	89	3	5	41	27	.271
1942	SLB	29	74	11	21	6	0	1	10	3	1	4	2	.284
1946	SLB	144	582	70	154	29	5	5	68	2	4	34	58	.265
1947	SLB	90	306	29	80	22	1	1	20	6	5	44	26	.261
1948	CLE	66	147	19	28	5	1	2	10	0	1	27	16	.190
1949	CLE	50	116	11	23	6	1	0	13	0	-	14	14	.198
1950	TOT	44	136	13	29	3	1	1	15	0	0	20	11	.213
	CLE	4	5	1	2	0	0	0	3	0	0	1	0	.400
	PIT	40	131	12	27	3	1	1	12	0	0	19	11	.206
1951	SLB	39	119	13	27	7	0	0	13	0	1	17	18	.227
1952	TOT	54	88	7	11	4	0	0	6	0	1	14	14	.125
	CLE	35	32	5	3	0	0	0	2	0	0	10	8	.094
	PIT	19	56	2	8	4	0	0	4	0	1	4	6	.143
11 Seasons		912	3028	334	755	167	23	36	387	27	29	284	268	.249

.094, he was traded to Pittsburgh and retired after the season to concentrate on his acting career.

He supposedly began his acting career as a child actor in the *Our Gang* comedies, although there is no record of that. His first movie role came in the *The Winner's Circle* in 1948, followed by the baseball movie *The Kid from Cleveland* in 1949. Assorted roles in movies and television followed, but his big break came when he joined the original cast of *General Hospital* in 1963. He played Dr. Hardy until his death from pancreatic cancer in 1996. One of the highlights of the show every year was Berardino's reading of the Nativity story every Christmas.

"Everybody adored him," actress Rachel Ames told *The Plain Dealer* in 1998. "John was like a father confessor to everybody in the cast. He always had a cheery word and liked to tell funny stories. He was a great dancer and loved to ride horses. On breaks between acting, he would play catch.

"He always knew his lines and everybody else's lines. He watched the show very diligently, where some of us didn't. He followed the ratings very closely. He wanted us to beat *Guiding Light*. He was very competitive.... He always wished Dr. Hardy wasn't so square. He loved playing gangsters."

Ames, who starred as Hardy's wife, nurse Audrey Hardy, told the newspaper there was a picture of the 1948 world championship Indians on the wall in Berardino's dressing room.

"He wore his championship ring all the time," Ames told the paper. "It was gorgeous. His wife made it even more beautiful, putting in a giant stone. He was so proud of it. He was always talking about his baseball days. He was wonderful in reciting *Casey at the Bat* at cast parties."

Berardino has a star on the Hollywood Walk of Fame and also was inducted into the USC Athletic Hall of Fame.

WORKING FOR A LIVING

Today's athletes have it pretty good. The astronomical salaries they make should allow them to take care of their families for the rest of their lives. In addition, their playing careers serve as

Fiery pitcher Johnny Allen, shown in this 1938 photo, became a minor league umpire after his playing days with the Tribe.

entries to a number of sports-related jobs like coaching and/or broadcasting.

But it wasn't always so. Well into the 1980s, athletes needed to look for work after their playing days were over. Sure, they had long lists of contacts, thanks to their celebrity status, so they likely weren't pouring through the want ads. But once they took off their uniforms for the last time, most of them started reporting for duty from 9:00 to 5:00.

It seems like such a foreign concept now. Could you imagine LeBron James selling insurance after his basketball career is over?

But what happened to Cleveland athletes after they retired and left the area was a favorite subject of longtime *Plain Dealer* sportswriter and columnist Bob Dolgan. Dolgan created a niche for himself at the paper with his historical pieces, and some of his most popular stories were those in which he caught up with assorted stars and everyday players.

Dolgan never failed to include information about what the player was doing and where he was living, and a collection of those stories was made into a book, *Heroes, Scamps, and Good Guys,* published by Cleveland's Gray & Company in 2003.

Some of the most interesting tidbits in the book included the new professions of the former ballplayers. Fiery pitcher Johnny Allen, for instance, became a minor league umpire. First baseman Hal Trosky, forced into early retirement by migraines, worked on his farm, then sold it and made a living selling rural real estate.

Pitcher Al Milnar became a security guard at Fisher Body, center fielder Earl Averill returned to Snohomish, Washington, where he ran a motel and florist shop, pitcher Emil "Dutch" Levsen returned to Cedar Rapids, Iowa, and ran an ice cream and butter store before selling insurance and then going to work for the Ohio Department of Agriculture in Cincinnati.

> # TRIVIA
>
> What was Emil "Dutch" Levsen's claim to fame?
>
> Find the answers on pages 159–160.

Surely one of the saddest stories in the book concerns the late first baseman Luke Easter, who was murdered in Euclid, Ohio, in 1979. Easter, the AL Player of the Year in 1952 who was credited with hitting the longest home run in Cleveland Municipal Stadium at 477 feet, played his last season with the Indians in 1954. He spent another 10 seasons in the minor leagues. Once he retired, he got a job as a polisher at TRW in the Cleveland area. Eventually he became the union steward. Every week, he'd go to the bank in Euclid and cash the paychecks of some of his co-workers. On March 29, 1979, he was on his way back to work with $40,000 when two men shot Easter and took the money. One of them had been fired from TRW, so he was familiar with Easter's routine. Police captured the two men. One got life in prison; one got a sentence of 15 years to life.

More than 4,000 mourners visited the funeral home, and about 1,000 attended the funeral. Woodland Hills Park on Cleveland's east side was renamed Luke Easter Park in his honor.

SOLDIER BOYS

DOING HIS DUTY

The way Bob Feller tells it, he was driving his new Buick Century from Iowa to Chicago on the morning of December 7, 1941. He was planning to negotiate his contract for the 1942 season.

Then came the news that the Japanese had bombed Pearl Harbor.

Feller, the greatest pitcher in Indians history, knew immediately that everything had changed. He planned on enlisting in the navy, in spite of the fact that as his family's sole support because of his father's terminal cancer, he would be exempt from the draft. But he became the first professional athlete in the country to enlist in the wake of Pearl Harbor.

Initially, he served as a chief petty officer under former heavyweight boxing champ Gene Tunney, who was in charge of the navy's physical fitness program. But that wasn't enough action for Feller, so he volunteered for gunnery school and became chief of an anti-aircraft gun crew on the USS *Alabama* in September 1942. Over the next three years, the ship was awarded eight battle stars, one for each of its invasions.

Feller was discharged in August 1945. Two nights later he started against the Detroit Tigers, pitched a four-hitter, and won, 4–2. Pitching in the major leagues for the first time in nearly four years, he struck out 10 and walked five.

That seemed to answer the questions about whether he (or any of the stars whose careers were interrupted) could regain their form—and how quickly. Then again, there are questions about how much better he might have been had he not left—and how many more victories he might have had. In his 1990 book titled *Now Pitching, Bob Feller: A Baseball Memoir*, Feller refers to a statistical analysis by Ralph Winnie that projected Feller would have had 107 more victories, 1,070 more strikeouts, two more no-hitters, and seven more one-hitters, but it's not something he dwells on.

"It may not prove anything, but it made for a lot of talk in the 'Hot Stove League' in those days, and still does," Feller wrote in his memoir. "There's always the possibility that something else might have happened even if a world war hadn't come along. We could have been injured and missed a full season or slipped on a banana peel, who knows? But this much I do know: I never heard one baseball player who missed time out of his career because of military service complain about it."

It is difficult to imagine any of today's sports stars voluntarily leaving their careers behind to fight for their country. That's part of the reason why so many idolized former Arizona Cardinals defensive back Pat Tillman. Tillman graduated from Arizona State

DID YOU KNOW...

That Pat and Kevin Tillman received the 11th annual Arthur Ashe Courage Award presented during the July 16, 2003, ESPY Awards? The award, presented annually to individuals whose contributions transcend sports, was accepted by Richard Tillman, Pat and Kevin's younger brother. In 2002, the award honored Todd Beamer, Mark Bingham, Tom Burnett, and Jeremy Glick, four passengers who lost their lives September 11 on United Flight 93. Other previous recipients included Jim Valvano (1993), Steve Palermo (1994), Howard Cosell (1995), Loretta Claiborne (1996), Muhammad Ali (1997), Dean Smith (1998), Billie Jean King (1999), Dave Sanders (2000), and Cathy Freeman (2001).

with a 3.8 grade-point average and a marketing degree in three and a half years. He was the 226th pick (out of 241) in the 1998 draft and four months later was a starting safety for the Cardinals. He had signed a three-year, $36 million contract. But after the attacks of September 11, 2001, he forfeited his salary and enlisted in the Army Rangers, where he made $18,000. (His brother Kevin left the Indians minor league system to go to war with his brother.) Pat Tillman was killed by friendly fire in Afghanistan. The fact that the army has been accused of covering up the facts of Tillman's death make the story even more sensational.

As far as Feller goes, in the minds of baseball fans it is almost impossible to separate his baseball accomplishments from his service to his country. In July 2006, the U.S. House of Representatives unanimously passed a measure introduced by Steven C. LaTourette (R–OH) recognizing Feller for his military service and the 60th anniversary of his historic 1946 season, when he went 26–15 with a then-record 348 strikeouts and a 2.18 earned-run average and led the American League in wins, shutouts, strikeouts, games pitched, and innings.

"I would argue that 'Rapid Robert' Feller is a hero in every sense of the word, both on and off the field," LaTourette said in a press release accompanying the 2006 passage of the measure honoring Feller. "He remains completely devoted to his sport, to the Indians, and to our men and women in uniform. He is a wonderful and selfless American."

Added representative Dennis Kucinich (D–OH) in the press release, "Bob Feller epitomized everything we hoped our professional athletes could ever be."

For Feller, though, there's a difference between athletes and heroes.

"Real heroes are not athletes," Feller writes in *Bob Feller's Little Black Book of Baseball Wisdom*. "Athletics and real heroes do not go together, except in the vein that an athlete should always maintain his dignity. The real heroes to me are those who served in the military and didn't return home. A real hero could be a Nobel Prize winner, a famous physician, a scientist, a policeman, or a fireman. Heroes are individuals who have done something to save lives. Athletes don't save lives. Athletes seldom put their lives at risk. At best, athletes could be role models in an athletic context.... Ballplayers seldom give up their lives to preserve ideals.

"There's nothing glamorous about war. The real heroes of World War II, the real heroes of any war, are the ones who didn't return. The survivors were the lucky ones, the ones who returned, such as myself. We lost more than 405,000 men in action defending our democracy in World War II. That doesn't even compare to how many men the Russians lost, or the British, or all the Allies for that matter. For me, it was an extra traumatic event because my father was dying of brain cancer at the time. I was young, impressionable, and deeply saddened by the casualties of war."

While Feller remains active in the Cleveland baseball scene, he also has continued his ties with the military. In March 2000, he became an honorary member of the Green Berets, in recognition of his work for the U.S. troops in Vietnam in 1969.

"There are only a handful of Green Berets in the world, and it fills me with great honor and pride to be one of them," Feller wrote in *Bob Feller's Little Black Book of Baseball Wisdom*.

HE LIVED TO TELL ABOUT IT

Gene Bearden is one of those players who would qualify as a hero in Bob Feller's book.

Yes, he was an athlete, a rookie pitcher who was one of the keys to the Indians winning the 1948 World Series. In fact, since he won the one-game playoff against the Boston Red Sox that allowed the Indians to advance to the World Series, you could argue he was the key. For his efforts, Bearden was voted the Indians' Man of the Year in 1948, the only rookie so honored— and considering his teammates that season, it was quite an honor.

"Winning the pennant was the culmination of a whole lot of hard work and a lot of dreams for all of us," he told author Russell Schneider in *The Boys of the Summer of '48*. "When you work all your life toward a goal, and then you reach it, you figure, 'This is

Gene Bearden, center, embraces his teammates—starting pitcher Bob Lemon, left, and catcher Jim Hegan—as they celebrate in the dressing room after winning the World Series in Boston on October 11, 1948.

what I set out to do when I was just a kid,' which I did, when I was 12 years old."

But he also was a war hero, even if he didn't often like to talk about it.

"Our ship was sunk," he told Schneider. "I was injured, but not enough to kill me. I was lucky, but anybody who got home was lucky.

"If I had my way about it, nothing more would ever be written about my experiences in the navy. I was just another sailor, luckier than many, because I met up with a doctor who, to me, was the best orthopedic surgeon in the business. His name was Dr. Wyland. I don't remember his first name."

Bearden was born on September 5, 1920, in Lexa, Arkansas, and grew up a St. Louis Cardinals fan. He was just 18 when the Philadelphia Phillies signed him for $250 and assigned him to

Class D Moultrie, Georgia, in the Georgia–Florida League. When a number of rainouts made a mess of the pitching rotation, his manager asked for volunteers to toe the mound, and Bearden stepped up. He did not make much of a first impression. His first pitch hit the batter in the neck. But he stuck with it and developed a knuckleball that carried him through his next four seasons, eventually moving to the New York Yankees organization.

Then in 1943 he joined the navy. He was a machinist's mate aboard the USS *Helena*, which was hit by Japanese torpedoes and sunk in the South Pacific near the Solomon Islands on July 6, 1943.

The front-page headline in *The Plain Dealer* the next day read, "U.S. Reports 6 Jap Warships Sunk," and notes the loss of one U.S. cruiser. "The first big sea victory in the week-old Pacific offensive was scored the night of July 5 and in the early morning hours of July 6 in the narrow body of water between New Georgia and Kolombangara Islands," the story read.

It would be almost five years later that Bearden told the paper what happened to him on that fateful day. According to the story that appeared on May 9, 1948, the day after his first major league victory, Bearden was in the ship's engine room when the first torpedo struck. Following instructions to abandon ship, Bearden was climbing a metal ladder out of the engine room when a second torpedo struck. He fell to the floor, his knee crushed and his head cut open by flying debris. He was unconscious.

"Somebody pulled me out," he told the paper. "They told me later it was an officer. I don't know how he did it. The ship went down in about 17 minutes. All I know is that I came to in the water some time later."

For the next two days, Bearden slipped in and out of consciousness, drifting in a rubber life raft with some other survivors until a U.S. destroyer finally arrived. Bearden was shipped back to the United States and had surgery at a naval hospital near Jacksonville, Florida. Doctors inserted a screw and an aluminum plate in his knee, and put another aluminum plate in the back of his head. He was told he'd never pitch again.

"I don't know how many doctors told me that," Bearden told the paper. "I didn't know what to do. I had learned a trade in the

A CHANGE OF POSITION

It might be a bit of a stretch, but one could make the case that if Bob Lemon had not joined the navy, he wouldn't be in the Hall of Fame.

Lemon, born on September 22, 1920, in San Bernardino, California, was signed by the Indians in 1938 as a third baseman and quickly established himself in the minor leagues. At New Orleans of the Southern Association, he hit .309 in 1939. At Wilkes-Barre of the Eastern League he hit .301 in 1941. At Baltimore of the International League he hit .268 with 21 home runs in 1942.

Then he went into the navy from 1943–45, where he occasionally pitched against other servicemen. When he returned, he faced one big obstacle as far as his baseball career was concerned: the Indians already had an All-Star third baseman in Ken Keltner. Manager Lou Boudreau tried Lemon in center field, but he stopped hitting. He reportedly was headed for the minor leagues when a couple of guys who'd batted against him during the war mentioned to Boudreau that Lemon had a pretty good arm. Boudreau had seen Lemon pitch batting practice, so he decided to see if Lemon had what it took to pitch in a game.

The 25-year-old right-hander started slowly as a reliever. He was just 4–5 with a 2.49 earned-run average the rest of 1946. But he went 11–5 with a 3.44 ERA in 1947, and he was off and running.

"He made the change so easy," Mel Harder, the former star pitcher who became the Indians' longtime pitching coach, told Bob Dolgan of *The Plain Dealer*. "He was such a good player that everything he did was right."

His trademark pitch was his sinkerball, and starting in 1948, when he went 20–14 with a 2.82 ERA and led the league with 20 complete games, 10 shutouts, and 293.2 innings pitched, he had seven seasons with 20 victories—a team record. He even won two games to help the Indians beat the Boston Braves in the 1948 World Series, which every long-suffering Indians fan knows was the last time the team ended a season victoriously.

"What would I have done if I had not switched to pitching?" Lemon said to author Russell Schneider in his book *The Boys of the Summer of '48*. "I don't know...but I probably wouldn't have lasted long in baseball."

navy, but baseball was the only thing I had known. Finally, I ran across a doctor who said he might be able to patch me up well enough. I think his name was Wyland. He was quite a guy. He worked with me for months."

Bearden told the paper his kneecap had been crushed and the ligaments in his knee were mangled, in addition to the gouge in his skull. After his operations, he spent a month in bed and then wore a cast for two more months. He graduated from crutches to a cane, but it was seven months before he could walk under his own power.

He wasn't released from the hospital until 1945, and then reported directly to the Yankees farm club in Binghamton, New York. Amazingly, he went 15–5 that season and then 15–4 the next season in Oakland before the Yankees traded him to the Indians, along with Al Gettel and Hal Peck, for Ray Mack and Sherman Lollar.

"The Yankees must have found out about my leg and traded me because of that," Bearden told *The Plain Dealer*. "We had to take physical examinations for the club and the doctors discovered that I had a plate and screw in my knee. I don't know whether they told Bill Veeck about it or not when they traded me. For all I know, neither Veeck nor [Lou] Boudreau knew about it, and I hope they're not mad when they find out. I've been treated pretty swell by Veeck and all the rest, and I don't want to do anything to get them down on me.

"Maybe I should have told them about it but I didn't want them to get the wrong idea before I had a chance to start. After all, it sounds worse than it really is."

It was unclear whether Veeck knew about Bearden's injuries before the trade. In Veeck's autobiography, there is no mention of them in his discussion of the deal. Rather, Bearden is one of several minor league pitchers under consideration to complete the trade. Veeck reportedly preferred Spec Shea but agreed to Bearden.

"The wild card here was the anonymous minor league pitcher," Veeck wrote. "One of the pitchers on his list was Gene Bearden, who was of special interest only because he had not played on a Yankee farm but had been on option to Oakland.

Casey Stengel was managing at Oakland, and I knew I could count on Casey for an honest appraisal. 'If [Larry] MacPhail's crazy enough to give him up,' Casey said, 'grab him.'

"I'm not going to say that I thought Bearden was going to be anything special. He was the biggest surprise I've ever had in baseball. The first year we had him, we sent him back to the minors. In 1948, though, he exploded. He won 20 games for us, including the playoff game against the Red Sox, and he pitched a shutout for us in the World Series and also came in to save the final game.

"It was the only good year Gene ever had."

It took awhile for the left-hander to make his mark. Though Bearden made the roster in 1947, he made just one appearance, giving up two hits and a walk to St. Louis on May 10, which left him with an earned-run average of 81.00. Still, when Bearden was sent down to Baltimore five days later, he put up a big fuss. He told the Indians if he wasn't going to play in Cleveland, he wanted to play for Stengel. Somehow the Indians pulled that off, and Bearden went 16–7 in 1947, setting the stage for 1948.

It was a great year, and it came at the right time for the Indians. He finished the season 20–7 and led the American League with a 2.43 earned-run average and six shutouts. He threw a five-hitter with six strikeouts to beat Boston in that playoff game, 8–3. Then in the World Series he beat the Boston Braves, 2–0, in Game 3 and saved Game 6 for Bob Lemon as the Indians won their second world championship.

In 1949, he went 8–8 and in 1950 was just 1–3 when Cleveland sold him to Washington. Stints with Detroit, the St. Louis Browns, and the Chicago White Sox followed but Bearden was back in the minors in 1954. He eventually retired in 1957 with a career record of 45–38.

"Gene Bearden was unique," Bob Feller wrote in *Now Pitching, Bob Feller*. "He came from out of nowhere in '48 to become one of baseball's star pitchers. He was with us the year before, but only long enough to have a cup of coffee, and there wasn't anything there to suggest that stardom awaited him the very next year.

"But Gene was working on something—a knuckleball. He started fooling around with it in the minors in 1946 and found the hitters didn't like it, which wasn't news to anybody. No batter likes to hit against a knuckleball pitcher. The ball has no spin on it and its flight is so unpredictable even the pitcher doesn't know where it's going. It's a 'butterfly pitch' that floats up there while bobbing and weaving in every direction imaginable.

"Everybody was rooting for Gene to make it. He had been badly wounded in the war in the engine room of the USS *Helena* in the Pacific. He was a star immediately in 1948, won 20 games and finished second to Jack Kramer of the Red Sox in winning percentage with 20 wins and only seven losses, a percentage of .741. It was a magic year for Gene, and he helped to make it so for all of us. But it was the only one of its kind for him."

After Bearden retired, he returned to Arkansas, where he worked at a radio station and later managed a storage facility. He died in 2004 at the age of 83.

"Indians fans will always remember his contributions to the team's last World Series title in 1948," team owner Larry Dolan said in a statement issued by the Indians upon Bearden's death. "His victory in the 1948 American League playoff game against Boston still ranks as one of the greatest wins in franchise history."

Indeed, in his book *Tribe Memories: The First Century*, author Russell Schneider calls that game "the Tribe's greatest victory."

PATRIOTIC ACTS

Patriotism is more difficult to define than it used to be.

Times were when flying the flag, saying the Pledge of Allegiance every morning at school, and cheering as the fireworks went off on the Fourth of July were signs of patriotism. Not many people do the first anymore, even fewer do the second, and as for the third, any connection between that holiday and the Declaration of Independence has been lost for most Americans.

The biggest spontaneous outburst of patriotism seen in this country in a long time came in 2001, in the wake of the attacks on 9/11, when stunned and heartbroken Americans scrambled to find those flags that had been stored in basements and attics, and

1945 ALL-STARS

The 1945 All-Star Game was canceled because of World War II, but *The Sporting News* still selected American League and National League All-Stars and printed them in the July 12, 1945, edition. One player from every team was selected, and the managers came from the 1944 World Series.
Indians who were named to the phantom All-Star team were Lou Boudreau, Frank Hayes, and Steve Gromek.

lawmakers sang an a capella version of "God Bless America" on the steps of the U.S. Capitol.

For those who were alive during World War I or II, patriotism was a more popular notion. Those wars seemed closer somehow, and they demanded more sacrifice from those at home. There was rationing of goods and services; there were air raid drills in an effort to keep us safe. Yet there was no debate over whether the United States should be involved. Veterans of those wars were welcomed home as heroes, and they continue to be recognized as such today. Even as their numbers dwindle as the population ages, there may not be a more patriotic category of Americans.

Of course, added to that group are those currently serving in the military and their families, especially those with loved ones stationed in dangerous situations overseas. Their concerns and sacrifices remain day to day. But for many Americans, the only time they think about the war is when they slap a yellow magnetic "Support Our Troops" ribbon on the back of their gas-guzzling imported SUVs. And what about the increasingly vocal opponents of the war? Though they support the troops, the government would have us believe that criticizing the war itself is unpatriotic.

This is not meant to fuel a political discussion or argument. It only sets the stage to discuss something that would be unheard of in our country today. In 1917, with the United States on the verge of entering World War I, the leagues ordered their players to undergo military training—using bats instead of guns. Not only were drill instructors eventually assigned to each team, but each team was graded on its drilling. According to author Russell Schneider, the Indians finished third in the American League.

As originally reported by *The Plain Dealer* on April 20, 1917, and recounted in Schneider's book, *The Cleveland Indians Encyclopedia,* the team strutted its stuff before beating Detroit, 8–7, on Opening Day at League Park. An account was displayed on the front page of the newspaper that day, under the headline "Flags Wave Our Tribe To Victory."

"Patriotic outbursts of applause, patriotic music and military drills which, for over an hour, kept 24,000 baseball fans in an enthusiastic uproar, finally quieted down and Old Glory, hanging limp on the pole behind the score board, for the time was forgotten, while fans gave all their attention to a baseball game," wrote James H. Lanyon, sporting editor of *The Plain Dealer.*

One feature of the afternoon which brought fans to their feet was the military drilling of the ballplayers. Directed by a uniformed soldier and carrying bats in place of rifles, the Detroit team seemed to have the edge on the home players so far as drill was concerned. Carrying something on their shoulders akin to a rifle made a tremendous amount of difference. But their applause was not a marker to the roar of appreciation that went up when Drill Master Tris Speaker led his Indians through their formations.

The Indians drilled well. You can't help but say that, but without their shouldered bats they did not appear so military. President [James C.] Dunn of the Indians expects to get an officer here soon to drill his team regularly, and then watch 'em.

The climax of the patriotic outbursts came when the players of the teams, headed by Kirk's band, marched around the field in military formation to the far corner of the field. Then, as the band played "The Star-Spangled

Banner," 24,000 fans stood up, the men removing their hats, and Old Glory slowly and steadily slid up the flag pole behind the scoreboard.

And there you are so far as patriotic enthusiasm went. In a minute the patriots were transformed into baseball fans of the most serious kind.

Take a minute to let that image sink in, and then fast forward to today. It is impossible to imagine Albert Belle marching in formation. The players association likely would file some sort of grievance, and pacifist fans would start a class-action lawsuit. This isn't like the huge flags carried onto the field for

HALL OF FAMERS IN WORLD WAR II AND THEIR BRANCH OF SERVICE

Luke Appling, Army

Al Barlick, Coast Guard

Yogi Berra, Navy

Nestor Chylak, Army

Mickey Cochrane, Navy

Leon Day, Army

Bill Dickey, Navy

Joe DiMaggio, Army Air Corps

Larry Doby, Navy

Bobby Doerr, Army

Bob Feller, Navy

Charlie Gehringer, Navy

Hank Greenberg, Army Air Corps

Billy Herman, Navy

Monte Irvin, Army

Ralph Kiner, Navy

Bob Lemon, Navy

Ted Lyons, Marines

Larry MacPhail, Army

Lee MacPhail, Navy

Johnny Mize, Navy

Stan Musial, Navy

Pee Wee Reese, Navy

Phil Rizzuto, Navy

Robin Roberts, Army Air Corps

Jackie Robinson, Army

Red Ruffing, Army Air Corps

Red Schoendienst, Army

Enos Slaughter, Army Air Corps

Duke Snider, Navy

Warren Spahn, Army

Bill Veeck, Marines

Hoyt Wilhelm, Army

Ted Williams, Marines

Early Wynn, Army

special ceremonies or singing "God Bless America" during the seventh-inning stretch.

For its part, baseball and other sports have done their best to honor our country and keep patriotism alive, especially for all those fans among the men and women in the armed forces whose favorite teams constitute a link to home and normalcy.

But the notion of athletes marching around the diamond in this day and age would be foreign to just about everybody, including Pat Tillman.

PAIN AND SUFFERING

UNSPEAKABLE TRAGEDY

Every franchise has its share of trials and tribulations—events that put the games in their proper perspective. An accident. An injury. An act of God with far-reaching consequences. No team is immune. Such incidents often create memories that remain longer than the outcome of any individual contest.

For modern-day Indians fans, such an incident occurred on March 22, 1993, the day pitchers Tim Crews and Steve Olin were killed and pitcher Bob Ojeda was severely injured in a boating accident on Little Lake Nellie in Clermont, Florida. Every Indian fan and everyone associated with the team remembers exactly where they were when they heard the news. Then–general manager John Hart and then-manager Mike Hargrove still struggle when talking about it.

Fifteen years later, the details remain as clear as they were on that horrible day. It was the team's only scheduled day off during spring training, a Monday. Crews, a free agent from the Los Angeles Dodgers, was in his first camp with his new team, along with his former Dodger teammate, Ojeda. He and his wife and three children had rented a house on the lake, which was about 30 miles west of Orlando. They invited the Olins and Ojedas for a day of relaxation. Patti Olin told friends later they got lost and almost turned back, but her husband wanted their kids to be able to go horseback riding so he pressed on.

A REPORTER'S NIGHTMARE

The Plain Dealer's Paul Hoynes will never forget the deaths of Steve Olin and Tim Crews.

"It was the hardest story I've ever covered," he said, referring to the boating accident that killed the two Indians pitchers during spring training in 1993.

Hoynes is a veteran newspaperman who is one of the best in his profession. But nothing in his long and distinguished career prepared him for the difficulty of that assignment. For one thing, as the longtime Indians beat writer, he knew Olin, who'd come up through the Indians farm system and spent four seasons with the parent club. So while it was his job to provide an objective report of what happened, it was impossible not to be affected.

Here, then, is one side of the story that hasn't ever been told before—the story behind the writing of the story.

"I remember when it happened, it was weird," Hoynes said. "It was a Monday night. I was done writing. I was talking to Dan O'Dowd, the assistant general manager then, working on some story, and he got off the phone real quick. He had to go, like it was some emergency. But that was five hours before I heard anything.

"I went back to the condo I was staying in. My dad and my uncle were visiting. It came across the TV. ESPN said there had been a boating accident and three Indians pitchers were hurt. They didn't know a lot. It just so happened that a bunch of Indians players were staying downstairs in the same complex. So I went downstairs and heard about it.

"The office told me to write something. I sat down and I couldn't write anything. I was just sitting in front of the computer. So I called the office and said, 'Let me dictate it to you.' I'd never written anything like that. I just looked at the computer thinking, 'How the hell do I write this?'

"So I got through that, but it kept playing on my mind all night. I woke my uncle up—he's good with maps—and I asked him, 'Where is this place? Clermont?' He showed it to me. It was like 3:00 in the morning. So I drove up there. I thought, 'I've got to find out where this place is.' It wasn't that far from Winter Haven, but it was in the backwoods of Florida. I was driving around all these weird lakes and I finally found it. I remember looking at the boat. It had been dragged out of the water. There was a cop car there, and a TV crew.

"I walked out onto the dock. You know those big, long ocean docks they have going into the ocean with a big *L* at the end? That what this dock was, but it was in this little puddle. This was Little Lake Nellie. It wasn't Lake Nellie. I thought, 'What is this huge dock doing here?' I think a handicapped person put it in. So I walked all the way out and I saw where it hit. Man, that just blew me away.

"They had a press conference the next day or the day after, and they brought all the relievers in, and they were talking about Olin and Crews. I just put my head down and cried. I couldn't even take notes. God, it was so sad. Then they brought Mike Hargrove and Patti Olin in. Geez, oh, man, it was terrible. All I remember about that two weeks was writing story after story. They sent [*Plain Dealer* news reporter] James McCarty down. They sent [*Plain Dealer* columnist] Bud Shaw down finally. That saved my life. I was ready to jump off the dock.

"I just remember sitting up in that press box in Winter Haven writing all day and all night. The bugs would be crawling all over because it's an open press box right next to a lake.

"I remember the next day after the accident all the national baseball writers were coming in. They wouldn't let anybody in the locker room. We were all standing in the parking lot. A couple of the clubhouse guys were bringing these big cardboard boxes out. One of the New York guys said, 'I bet that's the clothes from the dead players, because that's what they did with Thurman Munson's stuff.'

"I remember Mike Hargrove or somebody told us not to go near the players or to ask any questions. But the players were staying where I was staying. The Olins were staying there. I knew Olin the best. Crews and Ojeda, it was their first spring training. But Olin was a fun guy. I used to do a thumbs-up or thumbs-down every game. He always wanted to know when I came down after the game, 'Hey, thumbs-up or thumbs-down?'

"I went and knocked on the door, and they said Patti didn't want to talk. I was fine with that. I talked to some of the players who lived there. Hargrove got really mad at me. I asked him a question about who was going to close and he blew me off. So Bud went and talked to him. Bud told him, 'Would you rather have [Hoynes] doing it or some guy from the news side who doesn't know anybody?' That kind of got Mike straightened out. But I remember feeling really bad about it.

"Finally, we found out about a week later that Crews was legally drunk. I mean, it wasn't like he was falling-down drunk. He wasn't that much over the limit. I think it was a Friday night. We'd just gotten done writing our regular stuff. Bud said, 'Hey, we've got to write this.' So I sat down to write it and I could not write it. I was just burned out. Bud wrote the story for me. I was fried.

"I didn't go to the memorial service. I was writing.

"I still think about that. They planted these two trees at Winter Haven for Olin and Crews. I just wonder what they're going to do with that when they move. There's a plaque for them. I think they should put it in the new monument park in center field at Jacobs Field.

"It's something you never forget. I just remember walking to the end of that pier and seeing how long and far and big that pier was and how little the lake was.

"Kevin Wickander, a left-hander who was really tight with Olin, freaked over it. They had to trade him. They made a locker for Olin on every road trip. He sat next to it. Finally, he couldn't pitch. He couldn't get it out of his head. They traded him to the Reds. That was another casualty.

"Ojeda talked about wanting to commit suicide. Hargrove had a chance to play a game that day against the Dodgers, who'd been rained out. But Hargrove said his guys needed a break. He really beat himself up for that.

"It was bad."

After a fun day, the three pitchers decided to go fishing in Crews' 18-foot bass boat. It was about 7:15 PM, just starting to get dark. Although Crews was said to be familiar with the lake, the boat crashed into a new, unlit dock at a high rate of speed. They'd been on the water no more than 10 minutes. Olin, 27, who had been riding in the front of the boat, was killed instantly. Crews, 31, died the next morning. Tests later indicated his blood-alcohol level was 0.14, over the then-legal limit of 0.10. Ojeda, 35, was hospitalized with a severe scalp wound.

Families and friends grieved in private. Teammates had to mourn in public, as did media members who'd come to know the players and still had to relay the news.

Very few players could think of anything to say to the reporters the day after the accident.

"It's been a hard day," said catcher Junior Ortiz.

"I think everyone is still in a state of shock," said outfielder Glenallen Hill.

"You have to be strong to take something like this," said second baseman Carlos Baerga. "Right now, no one can talk. Everybody is down. We have to help the families."

Hargrove was the first member of the organization to hear about the accident. He received a call about 30 minutes after the crash from Fernando Montes, the team's strength and conditioning coach, who also had been at Crews's party. Montes was actually in the boat when the pitchers discovered they'd forgotten some gear. Montes, Olin, and Ojeda played the game "Rock, Paper, Scissors" to determine who'd get off the boat to retrieve the gear. Montes lost the game, which may have saved his life.

Hargrove met with reporters the day after the accident, but could not make it through the media briefing without breaking down. He had managed Olin in the minor leagues.

"Steve was more to us than just a pitcher," Hargrove said. "When things start flying around, you want people who don't look for holes. You want people who will stand up and take it with you. Steve Olin was that kind of guy. So was Tim Crews."

The team held a memorial service for Olin and Crews in Florida. Former Indian Andre Thornton, who lost his wife and daughter in a car accident in 1977, spoke.

"I didn't know Steve and Tim personally, but I played against Bob Ojeda," Thornton told reporters before the service. "As any fan, and as any former player, you feel a sadness any time two young men lose their lives. I certainly, along with other people in the city and the organization, feel that sadness.

"The brevity of life is a reality that life is short for some; it's shorter for others. There's always a great deal of hope that our faith gives us. Hope and encouragement begins the healing process. It really deals with our faith and it carries us through some of those situations in life."

The Indians' first concerns were with the families of Olin and Crews. The team established a memorial fund.

But as the shock of the tragedy wore off, there was a season to prepare for—and a huge hole in the bullpen to fill. On the same day he struggled to gather players' reactions, *Plain Dealer* reporter Paul Hoynes was called upon to write an objective analysis of what the accident meant to the team's bullpen. In his inimitable style, Hoynes mixed in just enough emotion before dealing with the difficult task of replacing Olin and Crews.

"Little Lake Nellie isn't much bigger than a puddle," he wrote. "It is a puzzling place for two men and a pitching staff to die.

DID YOU KNOW...

That after the accident manager Mike Hargrove never again gave his teams a day off during spring training?

BOB OJEDA (AFTER THE ACCIDENT)

1993 CLE   2–1, 43IP, 48H, 22R, 21BB, 27K, 4.40 ERA
1994 NYY   0–2, 3IP, 11H, 8R, 6BB, 3K, 24.00 ERA

"At 4:00 AM, disfigured slightly by the wind, it looks like a sheet of black glass. Harmless, really. What could there be to fear out there?"

After paying tribute to Olin, Crews, and Ojeda, who would eventually come back in August and finish with a 2–1 record and 4.44 ERA, Hoynes proceeded to look at the rest of the pitchers in the Indians farm system. In the middle of the story, where he was discussing long relievers, is a one-line paragraph: "Left-hander Cliff Young might be able to help them there."

In fact, Young would finish the season 3–3 with a 4.62 ERA and 31 strikeouts. But he was killed in a car crash in Texas on November 4.

A season that began in tragedy ended in tragedy, too.

A DEADLY PITCH

Sadly for the Indians, it was not their only experience with tragedy. On August 16, 1920, star shortstop Ray Chapman was hit in the head by a pitch thrown by Carl Mays of the New York Yankees at the Polo Grounds in New York and died the next day. He remains the only major league player ever fatally wounded during a game.

It was the first pitch from Mays in the top of the fifth inning, and it struck Chapman near the left temple. He collapsed on the spot, and umpire Tom Connolly immediately called to the stands for a physician. When Chapman regained consciousness, he was helped to his feet and eventually was able to walk off the field supported between two teammates. However, as he approached the dugout, he seemed to collapse again, according to newspaper accounts. Though he was unable to speak at the time, the next day *The Plain Dealer* reported that he was speaking that night at the hospital, which seems unlikely.

In *The Cleveland Indians Encyclopedia*, Jack Graney, former outfielder who was Chapman's roommate, said, "I helped carry [Chapman] to the clubhouse in center field, and I stayed with him until the ambulance came. He was conscious. He looked at me and tried to speak, but the words wouldn't come out.

RAY CHAPMAN YEAR-BY-YEAR

Year	Team	G	AB	R	H	2B	3B	HR	RBI	SB	CS	BB	SO	BA
1912	CLE	31	109	29	34	6	3	0	19	10		10		.312
1913	CLE	141	508	78	131	19	7	3	39	29		46	51	.258
1914	CLE	106	375	59	103	16	10	2	42	24	9	48	48	.275
1915	CLE	154	570	101	154	14	17	3	67	36	15	70	82	.270
1916	CLE	109	346	50	80	10	5	0	27	21	14	50	46	.231
1917	CLE	156	563	98	170	28	13	2	36	52		61	65	.302
1918	CLE	128	446	84	119	19	8	1	32	30		84	46	.267
1919	CLE	115	433	75	130	23	10	3	53	18		31	38	.300
1920	CLE	111	435	97	132	27	10	3	49	13	9	52	38	.303
9-year totals		1051	3785	671	1053	162	81	17	364	233	47	452	414	.278

"I knew by the look in his eyes that he wanted desperately to tell me something, so I got some paper and put a pencil in his hand. He made a motion to write but the pencil dropped to the floor. Paralysis was setting in. We found out later his skull had been fractured on one side, there was a concussion on the other side, and his neck was broken."

The Plain Dealer of August 17, 1920, reported that Indians manager Tris Speaker was optimistic despite fears of a fractured skull. Of course, the day after that the top headline was that Chapman had died and his body was en route to Cleveland.

Chapman, who was 29 when he died, was a native of Beaver Dam, Kentucky. He had a career .278 batting average from 1912–20 with 364 RBIs and 233 stolen bases.

But the statistics were not the only measure of the man. Chapman was a popular and much-respected player, and teammates and opponents mourned his passing.

"On the streets, in the subways, and wherever persons gather, the fate of the star shortstop, everywhere admired and respected, is being discussed....

"At the Hotel Ansonia, the local headquarters of the Cleveland club, the depression is pronounced," read one *Plain Dealer* story. "There one may see ballplayers walking idly through the corridors, their very action indicating that they are unable to realize that their pal and teammate is no more.

"Full-grown men, supposed to be beyond the realm of tears, wept today as they discussed the passing of one whom everybody regarded as a friend, and the whole team is stunned by the tragic occurrence....

"Every New York paper took occasion to pay a tribute of respect to a player who had been a credit to his profession from the day he first entered it. Several of the sporting writers had known Chappie personally but those who had not enjoyed his acquaintance recognized that he possessed qualities of sterling manhood that equaled his ability as a ballplayer.

"Tris Speaker was grief stricken. He denied himself to all interviewers and asked to be left to himself until he had partly overcome the shock which overwhelmed him when he learned that Chapman was dead."

Wrote Henry P. Edwards in *The Plain Dealer*, "There is a base-ball uniform with faint black stripes running through the while hanging in a locker at League Park. In the bottom of that locker is a muddy pair of baseball shoes. There is a cap on the top shelf with 'Chappie' written on the sweat band.

That Ray Chapman led the American League in walks in 1918 with 84?

"Never again will that uniform be worn. It is doubtful if that locker ever will be used again, for Ray Chapman, the star player who stowed his things in it and who was the wearer of that particular uniform, is dead....

"Chapman was a hardworking, earnest ball player and had a disposition that enabled him to chase away gloom that now and then hangs over every ballclub. He had a winning way that is possessed by few men. The players of every club in the circuit liked him. The rookies all swore by him. He had the personality that made friends and kept them. He did not have the power to make an enemy.

"Ray Chapman made traveling with the Cleveland baseball club a pleasure, for when the team lost a close game and was in the dumps, Chappie would get the quartet together and song would follow song and scores of travelers would gather around to listen, making up their minds Cleveland must have won that day.

"He also was a storyteller of ability and night after night when the Indians were on the road, he would entertain with amusing anecdotes of the diamond. He could tell them, too, so his listeners would laugh and laugh."

Even American League umpire Billy Evans wrote of Chapman, "In his death, Cleveland loses a real citizen: the Indians, a great ballplayer; and baseball, one of its finest characters. If there were more men like Chapman in baseball, umpiring would not be [a] half bad job. I know every member of the American League staff is mourning the passing of 'Chappy.' May his memory serve as an inspiration and a goal for those who aspire to be 'real genuine big leaguers.'"

While baseball mourned Chapman, it wondered about Mays. He had a reputation for hitting batters. In fact, he'd hit 55 since joining the league in 1915. After Chapman's death, members of the AL teams in Boston and Detroit wanted to start a petition to ban Mays. Nothing ever came of it.

In fact, Speaker told his players and reporters that he did not hold Mays responsible. That likely would have been exactly what Chapman said.

In a copy of his funeral oration kept by the main branch of the Cleveland Public Library, the Reverend Dr. William A. Scullen described Chapman as "ever kind, gentle, courteous, and whole-some...the friend that the soul is ever seeking....

"This was Ray Chapman, respected, admired, honored, loved, not only in this city but in all great cities of America.... The glory was his as a man. It still lives.... To other youths, may it be their fortune to play as fair as he did, may it be their fortune to die as he died, and as we say the last farewell, may the prayer that is in your hearts, the prayer that I trust will be there many times in the future as you remember him, be: May the soul of the gentle, kindly youth, who Heaven knows, rest in peace."

A CAREER CUT SHORT

Though Ray Chapman remains the only player ever fatally wounded in a baseball game, plenty of careers have been short-ened or ended by injuries suffered on the diamond. Herb Score's was one of them.

Score carried a can't-miss label when he made the Indians team in 1955. He already had survived some tough times by the time he started his career, and he wanted to put all of that behind him and look toward what appeared to be a bright future.

Born in Rosedale, New York, on June 7, 1933, Score was hit by a truck when he was three years old. His legs were crushed, and doctors told his parents he'd never walk again. But he recovered completely and also survived rheumatic fever a few years later. His parents separated when Score was a freshman in high school, and he and his two sisters moved to Lake Worth, Florida, with their mother.

Score was just out of high school when he was signed by Indians scout Cy Slapnicka, who had discovered Feller sixteen years earlier. By 1954, Score, playing for Indianapolis, was the Most Valuable Player in the American Association with a 22–5 record and 2.62 ERA with 330 strikeouts in 251 innings. The Indians brought him up in 1955, and he went 16–10 with a 2.85 ERA, striking out 245 batters to lead the AL and set a rookie record that stood until 1984, when it was broken by Dwight Gooden. In 1956, Score went 20–9 with a 2.53 ERA and a league-leading 263 strikeouts. In his first two seasons, the left-hander made the All-Star team twice.

TRIVIA

How many times did Herb Score lead the Indians in strikeouts?

Find the answers on pages 159–160.

He roomed with the popular Rocky Colavito. A couple of devout Catholics who walked the straight and narrow, the two were worthy role models for the youngsters who adored them.

But everything changed on May 7, 1957, when Score, just 23, was hit in the right eye by a line drive off the bat of Gil McDougald of the New York Yankees in the first inning of a game at Cleveland Municipal Stadium. Score, who never saw the ball, went down as if shot, and blood spurted from his eye, nose, and mouth.

"As soon as I hit the ground, I prayed to St. Jude," said Score, whose middle name is Jude. "I was afraid I wouldn't be able to see."

He told Hal Lebovitz of the *Cleveland News*, "I've been in pain before, but this is the worst. I feel like screaming."

Colavito rushed in from right field to check on his friend.

"When he was hit, his head was on the ground, and I put my glove under his head," Colavito said. "When the inning was over, I got to the clubhouse and Herbie said, 'What the hell are you doing here? You've got a ballgame to play.' That's something I've always admired about him. He handled it as good as anyone could."

Better, actually, than most.

At Lakeside Hospital, he granted an interview to *The Plain Dealer's* Chuck Heaton.

"That just shows you the type of guy he was," Heaton said. "Here he was in pain and he was thinking of my deadline."

McDougald was pained, too. He was terrified that Score would lose his eye. He tried to visit him, but hospital officials wouldn't allow it. He had to settle for frequent updates from the hospital on Score's condition.

"He threw it low and away, and I just flicked it," McDougald said. "The next thing I remember is watching Herb go down. All I recall is seeing blood. I don't recall running to first. I was very upset."

Score, 2–1 with a 2.00 ERA at the time of the injury, was in the hospital for three weeks and lost the rest of the season, but he returned in 1958. Unfortunately, his fastball was never the same, though he always blamed a torn elbow tendon suffered that spring and not the eye injury. He went 2–3 with a 3.95 ERA and 48 strikeouts in 1958 and was 9–11 with a 4.71 ERA and 147 strikeouts in 1959. He was traded to Chicago for pitcher Barry Latman on April 18, 1960, a day after Colavito was traded to Detroit. Score actually thought he was going to Detroit with Colavito until a bad outing in spring training probably caused the Tigers to change their minds.

DID YOU KNOW...

That the first pitcher the Indians lost under tragic circumstances was Addie Joss, who died of tubercular meningitis on April 14, 1911? He was 31. He was 160–97 with one perfect game, one no-hitter, and five one-hitters in nine seasons. The Veterans Committee waived the 10-year rule required for election to the Hall of Fame and inducted Joss in 1978.

HERB SCORE YEAR-BY-YEAR

Year	Team	W	L	IP	H	R	BB	SO	ERA
1955	CLE	16	10	227.3	158	85	154	245	2.85
1956	CLE	20	9	249.3	162	82	129	263	2.53
1957	CLE	2	1	36.0	18	9	26	39	2.00
1958	CLE	2	3	41.0	29	19	34	48	3.95
1959	CLE	9	11	160.7	123	93	115	147	4.71
1960	CHW	5	10	113.7	91	54	87	78	3.72
1961	CHW	1	2	24.3	22	19	24	14	6.66
1962	CHW	0	0	6.0	6	3	4	3	4.50
8-year totals		55	46	858.3	609	364	573	837	3.36

Score went 6–12 with the White Sox from 1960–62 before retiring.

"If Herb hadn't gotten hurt, he would have been as good as Sandy Koufax," Feller once said.

When the Indians asked Score to fill in on some television broadcasts in 1963, he took them up on their offer and stayed for the next 34 years, retiring after the 1997 World Series.

Meanwhile, McDougald left baseball not long after the incident, retiring in 1960 at the age of 32. "I really didn't feel like playing anymore," McDougald said in *The Cleveland Indians Encyclopedia*. "It took a few hitches out of me as a ballplayer, even though I know you can't control where the ball is going after you hit it. Everybody, including Herb's mother, tried to tell me it wasn't my fault."

In fact, Score never blamed McDougald. When the two met up years later, Score told McDougald, "I should have ducked."

Score suffered a number of medical setbacks after his retirement in 1997. A year later, he was severely injured in an automobile accident in New Philadelphia, Ohio, about 80 miles south of Cleveland. On his way to Florida, where he and his wife, Nancy, spend their winters, Score pulled out in front of a tractor-trailer, which hit him broadside. Score suffered bruises to his brain and lungs, cuts on his face, a broken bone above his eye, and three broken ribs. He recovered from that, but suffered a stroke. Then he fell and broke his shoulder and got a staph infection. When inducted into the Indians Hall of Fame in the summer of 2006, he was in a wheelchair and unable to speak publicly.

But whether fans remember him as a pitcher or broadcaster, there's no doubt they remember him.

"For 30 years minimum, he was the most identifiable Cleveland Indian," said current Indians radio announcer Tom Hamilton. "For a 30-year stretch, ownership changed constantly, players changed constantly. Whenever you had a good player, he didn't stay here. But the one constant was always Herb. For a good 30 years, if you said 'Cleveland Indians,' I think the first person people thought of was Herb. He was always there through thick and thin."

Added former Indians manager Mike Hargrove, "With any franchise, there are faces from the past and present that represent who they are as a team," Hargrove said before the ceremony. "I think Herbie is one of those guys, along with Bob Feller, Larry Doby, and people like that."

As if to prove the point, on the morning of May 7, 2007, on the 50th anniversary of McDougald's hit meeting Score's eye, *The Plain Dealer* featured a story and a photograph that showed Score with his right eye and head wrapped in bandages.

ANSWERS

Page 6: Hall of Famer Chuck Klein of Philadelphia is the only other major league player besides Grady Sizemore to hit 50 doubles, 10 triples, 20 homers, and 20 steals in the same season. Klein accomplished the feat in 1932.

Page 9: The Series was to have started in Cleveland, but renovations to the ballpark then called Dunn Field in honor of new team president Jim Dunn were not completed in time, so the first games were moved to Brooklyn.

Page 18: The only shortstop with more Gold Gloves than Omar Vizquel is Ozzie Smith, who has 13.

Page 31: Second baseman Tony Fernandez made the error that put Craig Counsell on base in the eleventh inning of Game 7 against the Florida Marlins.

Page 58: Steve Stone of the Chicago White Sox gave up Duane Kuiper's only home run in 1977.

Page 69: In 1987, Don Mattingly of the New York Yankees set the major league record for grand slams in a season (six) that Travis Hafner tied in 2006.

Page 73: Bob Feller's professional debut was on July 19, 1936, in relief at Washington.

Page 80: The victory went to John Rocker (5–6), who struck out the side in the eleventh.

Page 90: The 1969 Indians were 3–17 to start the season.

Page 106: Larry Doby, the former Indians star who was passed over by the team when it hired Frank Robinson, was the second African American manager in baseball, hired by the Chicago White Sox in 1978.

Page 127: Emil "Dutch" Levsen was the last pitcher to pitch all 18 innings of a doubleheader and win two games against the Boston Red Sox in Fenway Park on August 28, 1926.

Page 154: Herb Score led the Indians in strikeouts three times—1955 (245), 1956 (263), and 1959 (147).

NOTES

THE GOOD

"To watch him play day in and day out...." Tom Verducci, "One Sizemore Fits All," *Sports Illustrated,* May 14, 2007.

"He's the kind of player every manager wants...." Tom Verducci, "One Sizemore Fits All," *Sports Illustrated,* May 14, 2007.

"I didn't know what he was doing...." Tom Reed, "Trying stardom on for Sizemore; Young center fielder earns praise as player on the rise for Tribe," *Akron Beacon Journal,* October 9, 2005.

"You can never complain...." Tom Reed, "Trying stardom on for Sizemore; Young center fielder earns praise as player on the rise for Tribe," *Akron Beacon Journal,* October 9, 2005.

"I was at the All-Star Game...." Tom Verducci, "One Sizemore Fits All," *Sports Illustrated,* May 14, 2007.

"It's exciting...." Paul Hoynes, "Great news, Grady Sizemore named an All-Star, but Hafner must wait," *The* (Cleveland) *Plain Dealer,* July 3, 2006.

"It will be nice...." Paul Hoynes, "Tribe's review: Three stars, Sabathia, Martinez, Sizemore selected," *The* (Cleveland) *Plain Dealer,* July 2, 2007.

"I don't ever recall seeing Grady...." Tom Reed, "Trying stardom on for Sizemore; Young center fielder earns praise as player on the rise for Tribe," *Akron Beacon Journal,* October 9, 2005.

"I'm sure he'd be in the NFL...." Tom Verducci, "One Sizemore Fits All," *Sports Illustrated,* May 14, 2007.

"It was interesting...." Dennis Manoloff, "Battery confounds Phillies," *The* (Cleveland) *Plain Dealer,* June 19, 2007.

"You want it to last...." Paul Hoynes, "Blake contends beard analogy is razor thin," *The* (Cleveland) *Plain Dealer,* June 22, 2007.

"Coveleski pitched excellent ball today...." Staff Special, "Tribe's Hurlers Equal Dodgers', Speaker Says," *The* (Cleveland) *Plain Dealer,* October 6, 1920.

"I give Grimes the credit...." Staff Special, "Speaker Gives Grimes Credit for Box Work," *The* (Cleveland) *Plain Dealer,* October 7, 1920.

"The clubs are very evenly matched...." Staff Special, "Tris Confident Repeats Tribe Is Sure To Win," *The* (Cleveland) *Plain Dealer,* October 8, 1920.

"It was one of the most remarkable games...." "Proud of Every Indian in Game, Spoke Declares," *The* (Cleveland) *Plain Dealer,* October 1920.

"From the start, I never had any doubt...." "'I Knew it,' Said Speaker, as He Lauded Indians," *The* (Cleveland) *Plain Dealer,* October 13, 1920.

"Cleveland has a wonderful ball club...." "Robinson Doffs Cap to Speaker and His Indians," *The* (Cleveland) *Plain Dealer,* October 13, 1920.

"It was a tough one...." Charles Heaton, "Looks Forward To Being 'Back at These Guys'" *The* (Cleveland) *Plain Dealer,* October 7, 1948.

"I'm sure that Masi was out...." Harry Jones, "Lemon Seeks To Tie Series Today," *The* (Cleveland) *Plain Dealer,* October 7, 1948.

"Still no prediction...." Charles Heaton, "Doubles, Scores Tying Run, Drives Another Across," *The* (Cleveland) *Plain Dealer,* October 8, 1948.

"The toughest thing for me...." Charles Heaton, "Doubles, Scores Tying Run, Drives Another Across," *The* (Cleveland) *Plain Dealer,* October 8, 1948.

"Always wanted Gene to be a pitcher...." Charles Heaton, "Gene Declares He's Ready To Pitch Today and Will Be In Bullpen," *The* (Cleveland) *Plain Dealer,* October 9, 1948.

"We'll be back with Johnny Sain...." Charles Heaton, "Gene Declares He's Ready To Pitch Today and Will Be In Bullpen," *The* (Cleveland) *Plain Dealer,* October 9, 1948.

"I didn't sleep much last night...." Charles Heaton, "Lack of Sleep Fails To Slow Down Gromek," *The* (Cleveland) *Plain Dealer,* October 10, 1948.

"What a relief to get some runs...." Charles Heaton, "'We're On Our Way,' Declares Braves' Elliott," *The* (Cleveland) *Plain Dealer,* October 11, 1948.

"Oh, I was tired...." Charles Heaton, "Gene Plays Big Role In 10-Day Drive To Title," *The* (Cleveland) *Plain Dealer,* October 12, 1948.

"It was Bearden's series...." Charles Heaton, "Gene Plays Big Role In 10-Day Drive To Title," *The* (Cleveland) *Plain Dealer,* October 12, 1948.

"When I first saw Jacobs Field...." Omar Vizquel, *Omar!: My Life On and Off the Field,* Cleveland: Gray and Company, 2002, 73.

"I felt like I was flying...." Paul Hoynes, "Sandy Steals the Show," *The* (Cleveland) *Plain Dealer,* July 9, 1997.

"I kept his hitting streak alive...." Paul Hoynes, "Hargrove Praises Alomar's Defense," *The* (Cleveland) *Plain Dealer,* July 10, 1997.

"I've tried not to be a homer...." Paul Hoynes, "The Best I've Ever Seen," *The* (Cleveland) *Plain Dealer,* April 22, 2007.

"That would be awesome...." Mary Schmitt Boyer, "'Little' Vizquel Has Big Impact," *The* (Cleveland) *Plain Dealer,* June 10, 2002.

"The best thing I ever saw...." Paul Hoynes, "The Best I've Ever Seen," *The* (Cleveland) *Plain Dealer,* April 22, 2007.

THE BAD

"It was one of the most disappointing...." Dennis Manoloff, "GM frustrated with Friday's cold, sad ending," *The* (Cleveland) *Plain Dealer,* April 8, 2007.

"We were trying to get the game official...." Paul Hoynes, "Snow job does in Indians, Mariners get no hits, then get no game," *The* (Cleveland) *Plain Dealer,* April 7, 2007.

"When they finally called the game...." Paul Hoynes, "Snow job does in Indians, Mariners get no hits, then get no game," *The* (Cleveland) *Plain Dealer,* April 7, 2007.

"It was snowing as heavy then...." Paul Hoynes, "Snow job does in Indians, Mariners get no hits, then get no game," *The* (Cleveland) *Plain Dealer,* April 7, 2007.

"My wife [Amber] and I were standing outside taking pictures...." Paul Hoynes, "Snow job does in Indians, Mariners get no hits, then get no game," *The* (Cleveland) *Plain Dealer,* April 7, 2007.

"This is bizarre, absolutely bizarre...." Dennis Manoloff, "The Milwaukee Indians? Weather forces Tribe to play a long way from home," *The* (Cleveland) *Plain Dealer,* April 10, 2007.

"I wasn't expecting to hear 'Wild Thing'...." Paul Hoynes, "P L A Y B A L L. . .F I N A L L Y, Tribe wins 'Wild' one, Indians beat Angels in Milwaukee," *The* (Cleveland) *Plain Dealer,* April 11, 2007.

"Our next home game will be in Hawaii...." Paul Hoynes, "Indians chatter," *The* (Cleveland) *Plain Dealer,* April 12, 2007.

"Milwaukee has been fantastic...." Paul Hoynes, "Milwaukee farewell a blast Pronk's HR brings Indians home a winner," *The* (Cleveland) *Plain Dealer,* April 13, 2007.

"It was ridiculous...." Dennis Manoloff, "Welcome Home Again, Sort Of, Getting in game, not runners, Jacobs Field opener has Tribe stuck on bases," *The* (Cleveland) *Plain Dealer,* April 14, 2007.

"I can't wait until it's 90 or 95 degrees...." Paul Hoynes, "Restless Martinez back behind the plate," *The* (Cleveland) *Plain Dealer,* April 18, 2007.

"In 10 minutes...." Joe Maxse, "Indians on their game, so lost off-day no bother," *The* (Cleveland) *Plain Dealer,* May 22, 2007.

"I don't know if I was putting too much emphasis...." Dennis Manoloff, "No revenge for Byrd in loss to Seattle," *The* (Cleveland) *Plain Dealer,* June 12, 2007.

"The most important asset for a major league baseball player.... " Omar Vizquel, *Omar!: My Life On and Off the Field,* Cleveland: Gray and Company, 2002, 13.

"I can't tell you...." Paul Hoynes, "Marlins Win Game 7 in 11 Just Out of Reach," *The* (Cleveland) *Plain Dealer,* October 27, 1997.

"Nagy didn't lose this game, I did...." Russell Schneider, *The Cleveland Indians Encyclopedia, Third Edition,* Champaign, Ill.: Sports Publishing LLC, 2004, 494.

"I truly liked the man...." Hal Lebovitz, "Who can forget Lane?" *The* (Cleveland) *Plain Dealer,* March 21, 1981.

"No name invokes such utter, raw hatred...." Terry Pluto, *The Curse of Rocky Colavito: A Loving Look at a Thirty-Year Slump,* Terry Pluto, New York: Simon & Schuster, 1994, 33–34.

"I'm sure that the Indians knew...." Terry Pluto, *The Curse of Rocky Colavito: A Loving Look at a Thirty-Year Slump,* Terry Pluto, New York: Simon & Schuster, 1994, 34–35.

"Joe and I believe the home run...." Terry Pluto, *The Curse of Rocky Colavito: A Loving Look at a Thirty-Year Slump,* Terry Pluto, New York: Simon & Schuster, 1994, 48.

THE UGLY

"That's probably the closest we'll come...." Russell Schneider, "Stadium beer night fans riot, ending Indians' rally in forfeit," The (Cleveland) *Plain Dealer,* June 5, 1974.

"They were uncontrolled beasts...." Chuck Heaton, "Injured umpire: 'Like a zoo'," *The* (Cleveland) *Plain Dealer,* June 5, 1974.

"Billy called to thank us...." Russell Schneider, "Stadium beer night fans riot, ending Indians' rally in forfeit," *The* (Cleveland) *Plain Dealer,* June 5, 1974.

"I could see that there was sort of a riot psychology...." Russell Schneider, "Stadium beer night fans riot, ending Indians' rally in forfeit," *The* (Cleveland) *Plain Dealer,* June 5, 1974.

"Burroughs seemed to be surrounded...." Russell Schneider, "Stadium beer night fans riot, ending Indians' rally in forfeit," *The* (Cleveland) *Plain Dealer,* June 5, 1974.

"This was a mean, ugly...." Russell Schneider, "Stadium beer night fans riot, ending Indians' rally in forfeit," *The* (Cleveland) *Plain Dealer,* June 5, 1974.

"Those people were like animals...." Russell Schneider, "Stadium beer night fans riot, ending Indians' rally in forfeit," *The* (Cleveland) *Plain Dealer*, June 5, 1974.

"We expected trouble there...." Dennis Lustig, "MacPhail: 'No more beer nights here,'" *The* (Cleveland) *Plain Dealer*, June 5, 1974.

"I said things to him I've never said...." Bob Dolgan, "Belle Produced Summers of Fire, Fury," *The* (Cleveland) *Plain Dealer*, September 25, 2001.

"It's a very sensitive...." Amy Rosewater, "Selig Disappointed with Belle's Behavior," *The* (Cleveland) *Plain Dealer*, October 27, 1995.

"I loved him from 7:00 to 10:00 PM...." Bob Dolgan, "Belle Produced Summers of Fire, Fury," *The* (Cleveland) *Plain Dealer*, September 25, 2001.

"We had a great team...." Bob Dolgan, "Belle Produced Summers of Fire, Fury," *The* (Cleveland) *Plain Dealer*, September 25, 2001.

"Fans would call complaining...." Bob Dolgan, "Belle Produced Summers of Fire, Fury," *The* (Cleveland) *Plain Dealer*, September 25, 2001.

"They rolled out the red carpet...." Paul Hoynes, "Mound mayhem approaches futility," *The* (Cleveland) *Plain Dealer*, June 6, 2002.

"Our right fielder dropped...." Paul Hoynes, "Indians chatter," *The* (Cleveland) *Plain Dealer*, June 6, 2002.

"We just got the hell beat out of us...." Paul Hoynes, "Tribe beaten to a pulp," *The* (Cleveland) *Plain Dealer*, June 5, 2002.

"He couldn't throw a strike...." Paul Hoynes, "Tribe beaten to a pulp," *The* (Cleveland) *Plain Dealer*, June 5, 2002.

"You never feel sorry for the other team...." Paul Hoynes, "Tribe beaten to a pulp," *The* (Cleveland) *Plain Dealer*, June 5, 2002.

"We think we've got a good chance...." Russell Schneider, *The Cleveland Indians Encyclopedia, Third Edition*, Champaign, Ill: Sports Publishing LLC, 2004, 50.

IN THE CLUTCH

"It was typical Wicky fashion...." Paul Hoynes, "Classic Wickman earns saves mark," *The* (Cleveland) *Plain Dealer,* May 8, 2006.

"A year ago at this time...." Anthony Castrovince, "A familiar face pops up at the Jake, Wickman returns to Cleveland for the first time since July trade," MLB.com, June 16, 2007.

"Some guys say they don't turn it on...." Burt Graeff, "Wickman's work isn't just appearances," *The* (Cleveland) *Plain Dealer,* May 20, 2006.

"I had four great years with the Brewers...." Burt Graeff, "Wins Help Wickman Settle In," *The* (Cleveland) *Plain Dealer,* August 12, 2000.

"He's most effective...." Burt Graeff, "Wins Help Wickman Settle In," *The* (Cleveland) *Plain Dealer,* August 12, 2000.

"I liked the idea of going to Atlanta...." Burt Graeff, "Struggles give Inglett an inlet," *The* (Cleveland) *Plain Dealer,* July 23, 2006.

NUMBERS DON'T LIE (OR DO THEY?)

"Look, I'm just a guy from Peoria...." Burt Graeff, "Power Number Put Thome in Some Powerful Company," *The* (Cleveland) *Plain Dealer,* October 8, 1999.

"'Don't knock the Rock....'" Terry Pluto, *The Curse of Rocky Colavito: A Loving Look at a Thirty-Year Slump,* Cleveland: Gray & Company (paperback), 2007, 12.

"Everybody had a date...." Bill Livingston, "Hafner one to have and hold on to," *The* (Cleveland) *Plain Dealer,* July 20, 2007.

"He does fit Cleveland...." Bill Livingston, "Hafner one to have and hold on to," *The* (Cleveland) *Plain Dealer,* July 20, 2007.

"Gentlemen, I've found the greatest young pitcher I ever saw...." Franklin Lewis, *The Cleveland Indians,* New York: G.P. Putnam's Sons, 1949, 190–191.

"C.C. wants to be the man...." Russell Schneider, *The Cleveland Indians Encyclopedia, Third Edition,* Champaign, Ill.: Sports Publishing LLC, 2004, 244.

"I want to be a Roger Clemens type pitcher...." Russell Schneider, *The Cleveland Indians Encyclopedia, Third Edition,* Champaign, Ill.: Sports Publishing LLC, 2004, 245.

"I'm going to try to play...." Anthony Castrovince, "Sabathia ponders 300 wins, After Glavine reaches milestone, lefty considers his chances," MLB.com, August 6, 2007.

"I tried not to take it personally...." Bud Shaw, "Time not really on Tribe's side," *The* (Cleveland) *Plain Dealer,* April 5, 2001.

"It was a joy...." Anthony Castrovince, "Nagy, Thornton revel in Hall splendor," MLB.com, August 11, 2007.

IT'S NOT OVER 'TIL IT'S OVER

"The biggest lesson this game teaches...." Paul Hoynes, "Wow about that! Tribe rally erases 12-run deficit to stun Seattle," *The* (Cleveland) *Plain Dealer,* August 6, 2001.

"Back in 1994, 1995, and 1996...." Paul Hoynes, "Wow about that! Tribe rally erases 12-run deficit to stun Seattle," *The* (Cleveland) *Plain Dealer*, August 6, 2001.

"It felt like winning...." Bill Livingston, "Comeback salves woes of season," *The* (Cleveland) *Plain Dealer,* August 6, 2001.

"No doubt it was my biggest hit of the year...." Paul Hoynes, "Wow about that! Tribe rally erases 12-run deficit to stun Seattle," *The* (Cleveland) *Plain Dealer,* August 6, 2001.

"Kenny was pumped...." Tim Warsinskey, "Lofton caps comeback in memorable fashion," *The* (Cleveland) *Plain Dealer,* August 6, 2001.

"I got lucky...." Tim Warsinskey, "Lofton caps comeback in memorable fashion," *The* (Cleveland) *Plain Dealer,* August 6, 2001.

RACE RELATIONS

"I have always had a strong feeling for minority groups...." Bill Veeck, *Veeck—As In Wreck,* New York: Putnam, 1962, 171.

"If Jackie Robinson was...." Bill Veeck, *Veeck—As In Wreck,* New York: Putnam, 1962, 175.

Notes

"The acquisition of Larry Doby...." Thomas Joseph Moore, *Pride Against Prejudice: The Biography of Larry Doby,* Westport, Conn.: Greenwood Press, 1988, 42–43.

"For Larry Doby...." Thomas Joseph Moore, *Pride Against Prejudice: The Biography of Larry Doby,* Westport, Conn.: Greenwood Press, 1988, 50.

"People are doing a lot of unnecessary guessing," Gordon Cobbledick, "Plain Dealing There's No Need to Guess About Larry Doby; He Will Be Accepted if He Proves Big Leaguer," *The* (Cleveland) *Plain Dealer,* July 6, 1947.

"When I first went to bat in Chicago...." Thomas Joseph Moore, *Pride Against Prejudice: The Biography of Larry Doby,* Westport, Conn.: Greenwood Press, 1988, 57.

"It was one of the toughest things...." Bob Dolgan, "Tribe great Larry Doby dies, First black player in American League," *The* (Cleveland) *Plain Dealer,* June 19, 2003.

"It was an emotional time...." Bob Dolgan, "Memories stay fresh '48 Tribe center fielder Doby emphasizes the positive in a stories life of bittersweet baseball experiences," *The* (Cleveland) *Plain Dealer,* May 31, 1998.

"Color was never an issue with me...." Bob Dolgan, "A racial milestone Steve Gromek won a World Series game for the Tribe in 1948, but he is remembered for hug he gave Doby celebrating the win," *The* (Cleveland) *Plain Dealer,* April 26, 1998.

"I'm happy with the career I had," Bob Dolgan, "Tribe great Larry Doby dies, First black player in American League," *The* (Cleveland) *Plain Dealer,* June 19, 2003.

"Life is too short for that," Bob Dolgan, "Tribe great Larry Doby dies First black player in American League," *The* (Cleveland) *Plain Dealer,* June 19, 2003.

"I am happy that baseball...." Staff Special (Russell Schneider), "Disappointed Doby is not vindictive," *The* (Cleveland) *Plain Dealer,* October 3, 1974.

"After a great deal of difficulty...." Bill Veeck, *Veeck—As In Wreck,* New York: Putnam, 1962, 189.

"I think it would have been one of Jackie's biggest thrills...." Associated Press, "Jackie's widow happy," *The* (Cleveland) *Plain Dealer,* October 4, 1974.

"I'm the first one only because...." Russell Schneider, "Pitching top need, says Robbie," *The* (Cleveland) *Plain Dealer,* October 4, 1974.

"Frank Robinson is here because...." Russell Schneider, "Pitching top need, says Robbie," *The* (Cleveland) *Plain Dealer,* October 4, 1974.

"I don't see any problem in firing me...." Russell Schneider, "Pitching top need, says Robbie," *The* (Cleveland) *Plain Dealer,* October 4, 1974.

"I don't know if I could go through...." Russell Schneider, "Pitching top need, says Robbie," *The* (Cleveland) *Plain Dealer,* October 4, 1974.

"Frank Robinson is a man...." Hal Lebovitz, "Robbie...his time has come," *The* (Cleveland) *Plain Dealer,* October 3, 1974.

"I'm delighted somebody...." Dennis Lustig, "Reaction Generally Favorable," *The* (Cleveland) *Plain Dealer,* October 3, 1974.

"Frank is definitely ready...." Dennis Lustig, "Reaction Generally Favorable," *The* (Cleveland) *Plain Dealer,* October 3, 1974.

"I think it's a hell of a move...." Russell Schneider, "Tribe players endorse Robbie," *The* (Cleveland) *Plain Dealer,* October 3, 1974.

"If he manages the way he played...." Russell Schneider, "Tribe players endorse Robbie," *The* (Cleveland) *Plain Dealer,* October 3, 1974.

"It doesn't make any difference," Russell Schneider, "Tribe players endorse Robbie," *The* (Cleveland) *Plain Dealer,* October 3, 1974.

"Any home run is a thrill...." Russell Schneider, "56,204 see Robby's storybook debut," *The* (Cleveland) *Plain Dealer,* April 9, 1975.

"Right now I feel better...." Bob Dyer, "Robinson goes deep into baseball history; first black manager debuts with homer 30 years ago," *Akron Beacon Journal,* April 8, 2005.

"And even if you were frozen...." Hal Lebovitz, "Was it fiction?..." *The* (Cleveland) *Plain Dealer,* April 9, 1975.

"It was the kind of a debut...." Russell Schneider, "56,204 see Robby's storybook debut," *The* (Cleveland) *Plain Dealer*, April 9, 1975.

"More and more I'm realizing...." Frank Robinson, *Frank: The First Year*, New York: Holt, Rinehart and Winston, 1976, 167.

"I always did what I thought was right...." Russell Schneider, *Frank Robinson: The Making of a Manager*, New York: Coward, McCann & Geoghegan, Inc., 1976, 244–245.

"I'm not upset...." Russell Schneider, *The Cleveland Indians Encyclopedia, Third Edition*, Champaign, Ill: Sports Publishing LLC, 2004, 343.

"Dwarfing his teammates...." Brian McDonald, *Indian Summer: The Forgotten Story of Louis Francis Sockalexis, The First Native American in Major League Baseball*, New York: Rodale, 2003, 109.

"Many years ago...." Unsigned editorial, "Looking Backward," *The* (Cleveland) *Plain Dealer*, January 18, 1915.

TAKE THIS JOB AND SHOVE IT

"He certainly didn't let on to anything...." Louis Kaufman et al., *Moe Berg: Athlete, Scholar, Spy*, Mattituck, N.Y.: Main Road Books, 1974, 84–85.

"I never really saw Moe Berg...." Louis Kaufman et al., *Moe Berg: Athlete, Scholar, Spy*, Mattituck, N.Y.: Main Road Books, 1974, 84.

"It wasn't until years later...." Louis Kaufman et al., *Moe Berg: Athlete, Scholar, Spy*, Mattituck, N.Y.: Main Road Books, 1974, 86.

"Moe was a mysterious guy all his life...." Louis Kaufman et al., *Moe Berg: Athlete, Scholar, Spy*, Mattituck, N.Y.: Main Road Books, 1974, 85.

"I remember Moe did an awful lot of traveling...." Louis Kaufman et al., *Moe Berg: Athlete, Scholar, Spy*, Mattituck, N.Y.: Main Road Books, 1974, 85.

"I mailed the film to Washington...." Louis Kaufman et al., *Moe Berg: Athlete, Scholar, Spy*, Mattituck, N.Y.: Main Road Books, 1974, 98.

"I never had any indication...." Louis Kaufman et al., *Moe Berg: Athlete, Scholar, Spy,* Mattituck, N.Y.: Main Road Books, 1974, 123.

"I had no evidence that Moe Berg was a spy...." Louis Kaufman et al., *Moe Berg: Athlete, Scholar, Spy,* Mattituck, N.Y.: Main Road Books, 1974, 122.

"The most fun I ever had...." Bill Veeck, *Veeck—As in Wreck,* Chicago: University of Chicago Press, 1962, 133–34.

"Everybody adored him...." Bob Dolgan, "Two-Series Star After Helping the Indians to the 1948 Title, Berardino Found Fame as Soap Opera Actor," *The* (Cleveland) *Plain Dealer,* August 23, 1998.

"He wore his championship ring all the time...." Bob Dolgan, "Two-Series Star After Helping the Indians to the 1948 Title, Berardino Found Fame as Soap Opera Actor," *The* (Cleveland) *Plain Dealer,* August 23, 1998.

SOLDIER BOYS

"It may not prove anything," Bob Feller, *Now Pitching, Bob Feller: A Baseball Memoir,* New York: Citadel Press, 1990, 121.

"Real athletes are not heroes," Bob Feller, *Bob Feller's Little Black Book of Baseball Wisdom,* Lincolnwood, Ill.: Contemporary Books, 2001, 137–38.

"There are only a handful...." Bob Feller, *Bob Feller's Little Black Book of Baseball Wisdom,* Lincolnwood, Ill.: Contemporary Books, 2001, 138.

"Winning the pennant...." Russell Schneider, *The Boys of the Summer of '48,* Champaign, Ill.: Sports Publishing LLC, 1998, 132.

"Our ship was sunk...." Russell Schneider, *The Boys of the Summer of '48,* Champaign, Ill.: Sports Publishing LLC, 1998, 133.

"The first big sea victory...." C. Yates McDaniel, "U.S. Reports 6 Jap Warships Sunk," *The* (Cleveland) *Plain Dealer,* July 7, 1943.

"Somebody pulled me out...." Staff Special, "Bearden's Secret Is Out; Torpedo Can't Stop Him," *The* (Cleveland) *Plain Dealer,* May 9, 1948.

"I don't know how many doctors...." Staff Special, "Bearden's Secret Is Out; Torpedo Can't Stop Him," *The* (Cleveland) *Plain Dealer,* May 9, 1948.

"The Yankees must have found out...." Staff Special, "Bearden's Secret Is Out; Torpedo Can't Stop Him," *The* (Cleveland) *Plain Dealer,* May 9, 1948.

"The wild card here was...." Bill Veeck, *Veeck—As in Wreck,* Chicago: The University of Chicago Press, 1962, 144–45.

"Gene Bearden was unique...." Bob Feller, *Now Pitching, Bob Feller,* New York: Citadel Press, 1990, 150.

"He made the change so easy...." Bob Dolgan, "Indians recall 'great teammate,'" *The* (Cleveland) *Plain Dealer,* January 13, 2000.

"What would I have done...." Russell Schneider, *The Boys of the Summer of '48,* Champaign, Ill.: Sports Publishing LLC, 1998, 115.

"Patriotic outbursts of applause...." James H. Lanyon, "Flags Wave Our Tribe to Victory, Crowds Wild As Home Club Wins First Game," *The* (Cleveland) *Plain Dealer,* April 20, 1917.

PAIN AND SUFFERING

"It's been a hard day...." Paul Hoynes, "Tears hint at depth of sorrow," *The* (Cleveland) *Plain Dealer,* March 24, 1993.

"I think everyone is still...." Paul Hoynes, "Tears hint at depth of sorrow," *The* (Cleveland) *Plain Dealer,* March 24, 1993.

"You have to be strong...." Paul Hoynes, "Tears hint at depth of sorrow," *The* (Cleveland) *Plain Dealer,* March 24, 1993.

"Steve was more to us...." Paul Hoynes, "Tears hint at depth of sorrow," *The* (Cleveland) *Plain Dealer,* March 24, 1993.

"I didn't know Steve and Tim...." Tim Warsinskey, "Thornton to speak at service," *The* (Cleveland) *Plain Dealer,* March 24, 1993.

"Little Lake Nellie...." Paul Hoynes, "Deaths leave huge hole in pitching staff," *The* (Cleveland) *Plain Dealer,* March 24, 1993.

"Left-hander Cliff Young...." Paul Hoynes, "Deaths leave huge hole in pitching staff," *The* (Cleveland) *Plain Dealer,* March 24, 1993.

"I knew by the look in his eyes," Russell Schneider, *The Cleveland Indians Encyclopedia, Third Edition,* Champaign, Ill.: Sports Publishing LLC, 153.

"On the streets...." William Slocum, "Chapman Body Arrives Home Today," *The* (Cleveland) *Plain Dealer,* August 18, 1920.

"There is a baseball uniform...." Henry P. Edwards, "Ray Chapman Was Life of Cleveland Indians in Victory or Defeat," *The* (Cleveland) *Plain Dealer,* August 18, 1920.

"In his death...." Billy Evans, "Says Every Arbiter of League Mourns Player," *The* (Cleveland) *Plain Dealer,* August 18, 1920.

"As soon as I hit the ground...." Bob Dolgan, "A Sickening Thud," May 6, 1997.

"I've been in pain before...." Bob Dolgan, "A Sickening Thud," May 6, 1997.

"When he was hit...." Amy Rosewater, "Game's The Same, Four Decades of Broadcasting Baseball Still Brings An 'Oh My!' To Herb Score's Lips," July 8, 1994.

"That just shows you...." Amy Rosewater, "Game's The Same, Four Decades of Broadcasting Baseball Still Brings An 'Oh My!' To Herb Score's Lips," July 8, 1994.

"He threw it low and away...." Bob Dolgan, "A Sickening Thud," May 6, 1997.

"If Herb hadn't gotten hurt...." Russell Schneider, *The Cleveland Indians Encyclopedia, Third Edition,* Champaign, Ill.: Sports Publishing LLC, 245–46.

"I really didn't feel like playing...." Russell Schneider, *The Cleveland Indians Encyclopedia, Third Edition,* Champaign, Ill.: Sports Publishing LLC, 246.

"I should have ducked...." Amy Rosewater, "Game's The Same, Four Decades of Broadcasting Baseball Still Brings An 'Oh My!' To Herb Score's Lips," July 8, 1994.